Handbook of Miracles

To Father Freddy—
My favorite priest
who helped inspire
me write this book.

Nick Prerad
12-19-13

Handbook of Miracles

Nicholas Llanes Rosal, STD, PhL, MSJ

This book was printed in the United States of America.

Rev. date: 10/22/2013

To order additional copies of this book, contact:
Xlibris LLC
1-888-795-4274
www.Xlibris.com
Orders@Xlibris.com
139624

CONTENTS

Dedicated

to All Who Believe in Miracles

and Accept What They Reveal

Theological and Scriptural Bases of Miracles

Why Miracles?

SINCE HE NEEDED a larger lot for his church, St. Gregory Thaumaturgus commanded a mountain to move. The mountain moved. The Saint followed Jesus' words: "Have faith in God. Amen I say to you, whoever says to the mountain, 'Arise, and hurl yourself into the sea,' and does not waver in his heart, but believes that whatever he says will be done, it shall be done for him. Therefore, I say to you, all things whatever you ask for in prayer, believe that you shall receive, and they shall come to you" (Mk 11:23-24).

St. Gregory was born a pagan during the second century in Syria. Converted to Christianity through the work of the philosopher-theologian Origen, he became known for his edifying life, bringing thousands into the fold by his preaching and miracles. When he became bishop of Caesarea, he found only seventeen Christians there; but at the time of his death in 270, only seventeen pagans remained in the same city.

St. Gregory's miracles were only among thousands of miracles that have become part of the life of the church from Jesus' times to the present. Miracles have been distinct signs of Christ's love for

His followers as His church travels to its ultimate goal of becoming the New Jerusalem described in Revelation (Apoc. 14:14-20). *Man's salvation, the church's final triumph, and the proclamation of God's glory are the ultimate purposes of all miracles.*

What Are Miracles?

Miracles are observable, extraordinary facts or events that happen through divine intervention. They strike instantaneous fear (Mk 5:16, 7:16; Lk 2:9, etc.), awe, wonder, and admiration. They are not for entertainment as the mad King Herod wanted them from Jesus (Lk 23:8-9). Neither were they meant for the amusement of Satan, who tempted Jesus to turn stone to bread or to let Himself fall from the temple pinnacle so that angels could come down to minister to Him (Lk 4:13). *The extraordinary, awesome character of miracles is meant by God to attract man's curiosity to hear what He wants him to know or need to know for his salvation.* That's divine psychology—very much like what scholastics used to teach: learning starts with the senses. Indeed, once man's attention is engaged, God reveals his message—a salvation-related message. Thus, behind every true miracle is a message meant to guide man on his way to the ultimate purpose for which he exists: his eternal happiness in heaven. God uses miracles as his mediums, which, per se, are more powerful, more persuasive, and more attention-getting than any man's admirable, often entertaining communications technology.

Miracles are not fantasies created by man's fertile imagination. They are realities—real historic events—willed and caused by the Maker of the world. Recall the burning bush that excited Moses' curiosity? "Leading the flock across the desert, he came to Horeb, the mountain of God. There, an angel of the Lord appeared to him in the fire flaming out of a bush. As he looked on, he was surprised to see that the bush, though on fire, was not consumed. So Moses decided, 'I must go over to look at this remarkable sight and see why the bush is not burning'" (Ex 3:1-3). Then, God spoke to him, "I have witnessed the affliction of my people in Egypt and have

NICHOLAS LLANES ROSAL, STD, PHL, MSJ

heard them cry . . . I will send you to Pharao to lead my people, the Israelites, out of Egypt" (Ex 3:7-10). Past the miracle, God's message.

What Do They Mean?

Considering miracles as conveyors of God's messages, we see how God guided Israel and Christ's church through miracles. Divine revelations were preceded by miracles: the burning bush before God called Moses to lead Israel, the parting of the waters and the miraculous thunders of Sinai before God gave Moses the Decalogue, the sun and moon standing still before God let the Israelites defeat their idolatrous foes (Jo 10:13), and the collapse of Jericho's double walls before the Lord delivered the city to the Israelites as He had promised (Jo 6:1-3). Josue relates (6:3-4) a clear connection between miracle and revelation: "<u>This is how you will know that there is a living God in your midst</u> . . . When the soles of the feet of the priests carrying the Ark of the Lord . . . touch the water of the Jordan, it will cease to flow; for the water flowing down from upstream will halt in a solid bank" (4:9-13).

In the New Testament times, Christ was the miracle and revelation Himself. As the Son of God, He was the miracle of miracles. As the Word, He was the revelation revealed. As St. John explains, "In the beginning was the Word, and the Word was with God; and the Word was God" 11:23). What greater miracle could there ever have been than God Himself appearing to men in the form of man to reveal His divinity and everything man needs to know to reach his ultimate destiny? He was the source and, at the same time, the subject of revelation. He said, "I am the truth" (Jn 14:6)—the revealed truth to live by! Preaching and performing miracles, He gathered multitudes to show them the way to reach heaven. He taught about His kingdom (Lk 9:11), fed them, healed their sick, drove devils from their possessed, consoled them in their sorrows, and even forgave their sins. He trained a chosen group of men to spread His message after His ascension to heaven. From among them, He picked Peter on whom to build His church, against which the gates of hell would not prevail (Mt 6:19). He gave him the keys to His kingdom and charged him to feed His sheep (Jn 21:15-17). He gave him and the other apostles the power to forgive sins, promising that the sins would be forgiven. To continue tending His church unto the end of time, He established the sacraments by which He would pour His mercy on generation after generation of believers.

(Reflection: To keep His church as pure a gift to His Father as could be, He instituted the sacrament of penance whereby sins are effaced, souls purified, and their beauty restored. Penance also arms the soul against the onslaught of Satan, who continually tries to wrest it away from Christ. A wondrous miracle is Christ's Eucharistic presence in churches all over the world; the Blessed Sacrament in church tabernacles makes Himself accessible and public as He was on the streets and in homes and synagogues of Galilee. But even more awesome is His sharing of Himself—body, soul, and divinity—in Holy Communion! Didn't He say, "I am the bread of life. He who comes to me shall not hunger" (Jn 6:35-36)? As believers, we can say, "Give us always this bread" (Jn 6:34). This sacrament enhances the beauty of the soul and provides it with the food it needs on its way to eternity.)

After He ascended to heaven, He sent the Holy Spirit to teach and strengthen His followers. With the Spirit, He gave His church the gift of miracle along with other gifts. And He is still with us: "And behold, I am with you all days, even unto the consummation of the world" (Mt 28:20). That itself is a great miracle—a continuing miracle that started with His miraculous conception in the womb of Mary.

Miraculous Conception: Mary

Christ's miraculous conception in the womb of Mary was so remarkable that, together with His resurrection and ascension, it became part of the Creed. But even as we consider the miraculous conception of Jesus, we must not lose sight of the miraculous

NICHOLAS LLANES ROSAL, STD, PHL, MSJ

character of Mary's motherhood, which is part of God's plan of salvation. Because God, from eternity, had chosen her to be the mother of His Son, it behooved Him to endow her with an exceptional honor befitting her motherhood. He bestowed on her—from the first moment of her conception—*the fullness of grace that exempted her from all stain of sin.* "Hail, full of grace," Angel Gabriel addressed her so (Lk 1:28). *Grace*, in the teachings of Sts. Peter and Paul, meant a gratuitous friendship with God, a participation in the life of God (1 Pt 1:3, 4:13, 3:7; Rom 8:14-17; Gal 3:26). Mary's friendship with God was complete; she lived fully in Him. There was no room for sin in her, not even a stain, as the Latin hymn proclaims, "Macula non est in te" (There's no stain in thee). God would not allow His Son to be sheltered in a womb tainted by sin, would He? The immaculate nature of Mary's conception was *beyond* the process by which children of Adam are conceived blemished. As St. Paul said, "By the disobedience of the one man, the many were constituted sinners" (Rom 5:19). Therein lies the miraculous nature of *Mary's Immaculate Conception*: God *exempted her* from the universal, sin-infected conception of Adam's children. Declaring this miracle as a dogma of faith, Pope Pius IX proclaimed in 1854:

> The most Blessed Virgin Mary was, from the first moment of her conception, by a singular grace and privilege of Almighty God and by virtue of the merits of Jesus Christ, Savior of the human race, preserved immune from all stain of original sin. (Par. 491, *Catechism of the Catholic Church*)

By reason of her fullness of grace, for being the mother of the Son of God, and for her untainted purity, her Son—conqueror of death—did not let her decay in the grave. He glorified her and took her—*body and soul*—with Him to His abode. Untouched by sin, she was justly not subjected to sin's punishment. On Mary's assumption to heaven, the *Catechism* states:

> Finally, the Immaculate Virgin, preserved from all stains of original sin, when the course of her earthly life was finished, was taken up

body and soul into heavenly glory, and exalted by the Lord as Queen over all things, so that she might be the more fully conformed to her Son, the Lord of lords and conqueror of sin and death. (Par. 966)

(Reflection: The Catholics' trust in Mary as the most powerful intercessor among the saints is based on the fact that she is totally immersed in her Son's divinity. Hence, talking to her in prayer is, in effect, talking to Jesus Himself. A plea into Mary's ears becomes a plea into her Son's ears. Since there is only one divinity, one God, whatever Jesus hears reaches the ears of the Father and the Holy Spirit. Remember the wedding in Cana? A favor granted by Mary is a favor granted by her Son—the second person of the undivided Holy Trinity.)

Jesus' Miraculous Conception

Keeping in mind that miracles exceed nature, we recall how Angel Gabriel appeared to Mary. Addressing her with an extraordinary greeting, he said, "Hail, full of grace, the Lord is with thee. Blessed are thou among women." Mary was troubled by the unusual greeting but became even more troubled when she, knowing she was a virgin, heard the angel announce to her, "Behold, **thou shalt conceive in thy womb** and **shall bring forth a son** and thou shalt call his name Jesus. He shall be great, and shall be called **the Son of the Most High**." She knew that to conceive is within the realm of nature, but to conceive without another human being? Just impossible. In the ordinary process of human conception, nature requires that two humans contribute the elements that unite to form an embryo. So she asked, "How shall this happen, since **I do not know man?**" "And the angel said to her, 'The Holy Spirit shall come upon thee and the power of **the Most High shall overshadow thee;** therefore, **the Holy One to be born shall be called the Son of God.**'" *The father of her son is God?* Is that possible? Then, the angel gave her a sign (a miracle) to reassure her: "Behold, Elizabeth thy kinswoman also has conceived a son in her old age, and she who was called barren is now in her sixth month [barren and way past the ability to conceive?] **for nothing shall be impossible with God."** Then, Mary said, "Behold the handmaid of the Lord. Be it done to me according to thy word" (Lk 1:25-39). And so, it came to pass that Mary "conceived of the Holy Spirit," not of a man! Truly a miracle, infinitely beyond the requisite of nature!

The miraculous action of the Holy Spirit in Jesus' conception extended throughout Jesus' sojourn in Mary's womb until His birth. In consideration of the dignity of Mary as the mother of the Son of God, the Holy Spirit preserved not only her moral virtue of purity but also the integrity of her physical virginity. He allowed Jesus to come out into the world without violating His mother's *signaculum*, to use St. Thomas' term (2-2 q 152, 3 ad 3). For this reason, Catholics believe Mary remained a *virgin before*, *during*, and *after* Jesus' birth. But we ask, When Jesus was exiting from Mary, how could two physical objects (Jesus' body and the *signaculum*) be in the same place at the same time? That appears to be quite impossible. It's similar to what St. Thomas cited as physically impossible: two suns being in the same place at the same time—an example of the highest degree of impossibility nature can't do.

However, we recall how the disciples were gathered in a room behind a closed door "for fear of the Jews" when "Jesus came and stood in the midst of them and said, 'Peace be to you'" (Jn 20:19-2). How did Jesus enter the room through the wall? (Scholastic philosophers would attempt to explain that by citing their cosmological concept of matter, which is composed of internal and external quantity. External quantity [composed of physical mass], which is the extension of internal quantity, can be suspended, thus allowing the internal quantity [Jesus' body] to pass by another internal body [wall] without harming each other. Therefore, conceptually, one body in a given moment can be in the same place at the same time as another. Hence, suspending the mass of Jesus' body—which was done through a miracle—allowed His body to pass through the wall. In a similar manner, Jesus' body passed through the birth canal without violating the *signaculum*, thereby preserving the integrity of Mary's virginity.) Indeed, we must remember that when Jesus rose from the dead, He showed Himself as "the Lord of glory" (1 Cor 2:8), radiant with the power of God (Acts 15:8). To enter a room through a closed door or solid wall was a manifestation of that power. *Jesus possessed that same power that made Him come out of the womb of Mary without violating her physical virginity.*

The Son of God is the Word St. John wrote about: "The Word was with God; and **the Word was God . . . .** All things were made through him, and without him, was made nothing that has been made" (1:1-4). As God, Creator of everything, *only He possesses the power to perform miracles.* Throughout the gospels, we read how His miracles showed the perfect unity between His divinity and humanity. As the Word made flesh, He rules over angels, humans, and devils. He shows His unlimited power over nature: every element and potency embedded in it, every movement and every whit of time in it. He can make nature perform *above* and *beyond* its characteristic capability (as when a dead man, who is absolutely unable to bring himself back to life, rises from his lifeless state) or *beyond* their characteristic behavior (as when a raging storm that customarily takes days to clear instantly stops). Author of all things, God can stop the action of anything He created. Thus, as St. Thomas Aquinas concludes, *"miracles are singular happenings that occur **beyond** (praeter) the scope of nature. They **exceed** the capability of what nature can do or perform (Summa,* 1 q 105, 7 ad 2) . . . but always through God's intervention." For "things that are impossible with men (nature) are possible with God" (Lk 18:27).

Depending on the degree of potency a miracle exceeds, one miracle can be considered greater than another (1q 108, art 8). Bringing a dead person back to life is greater than restoring sight to a blind person. To some who cannot explain an extraordinary event, a phenomenon may appear to be a miracle. But as the Angelic Doctor notes, to others, like many scientists who may know the cause of an extraordinary happening, such an event is only a normal occurrence (ibid.).

Revelation and Miracles

Showing God's power were the many miracles wrought through Moses—the ten plagues in Egypt, the parting of the waters, the bursting fountain from the rock, the manna in the desert, and the possession of the Promised Land. These miracles and many more by the Old Testament prophets testified to God's love and mercy for His chosen people. They are an amazing allegorical *parallel* to how God, through countless miracles, lovingly guides and looks after Christ's church. Miracles confirmed the credibility of Moses and the prophets; the miracles enabled them to lead God's chosen people to the Promised Land. Jesus' own miracles confirmed His credibility among multitudes. Through and with His chosen followers down the centuries, He leads them—His church—to the eternal land of promise.

Keeping in mind that miracles are intended to convey divine messages, we recall how Moses' miracles led Israel (then in the midst of an idolatrous and polytheistic environment) to know and acknowledge *only one God* as their Father. Likewise, Jesus' miracles caused many to believe in Him. Among those numerous miracles, St. John tells us of a certain royal official whose son was lying sick at Capharnaum. "He went to him and besought him to come down and heal his son, for he was at the point of death. Jesus therefore said to him . . . 'Go thy way, thy son lives.' . . . . As he was going down, his servants met him and brought word that his son lives. The father knew then that it was at that hour in which Jesus said to him, 'Thy son lives.' *And he himself believed, and his whole household*" (4:46-53).

The entire household's believing in Jesus was a multiple conversion. Conversions (never without the work of the Holy Spirit) are interior miracles, according to St. Thomas Aquinas. They are externalized as visibly changed behavior—becoming public like other known miracles. Among other such miracles was the conversion of the thief on Jesus' right hand. After confessing his guilt and accepting what he called his just punishment, he prayed and acknowledged Jesus as his Lord: "Lord, remember me when thou comest into thy kingdom" (Lk 23:40-43). On the same occasion, another conversion took place amid miraculous happenings—darkness over the whole land, darkened sun, temple curtain torn in half—a centurion, standing and facing the dying Jesus on the cross, glorified God and confessed, "Truly this was a just man" (Lk 23:47-48).

(Reflection: The thief and centurion, among countless examples, show us the elements of a true conversion: faith in God, acknowledgment of sin against Him, recognition of just punishment that sin deserves, trust in His goodness, hope for mercy, humility to beg, resignation to accept God's will, adoration, and thanksgiving. These elements provide a pattern of how one can make his or her sacramental confession a true conversion. Also note how Jesus, although physically away from the servant, cured him. However far away Jesus may feel to us, let us have faith: He can answer our prayer from a distance!)

St. Peter's and St. Paul's Conversions

Among well-known miracles of conversion were those of St. Peter and St. Paul. When the Lord "turned and looked upon Peter, Peter remembered the words . . . 'Before the cock crows, thou will deny me three times" (Lk 23:40-43). *Remembering* Jesus' words was an enlightenment: a sudden recognition of his failing, his guilt (three times he had denied his master). They evoked remorse (regretting his denial—a change in attitude) that prompted him to go out and weep bitterly (externalization of his conversion). In the end, he would die for his master during Nero's persecution of Christians between AD 64 and 67.

In St. Paul's conversion, Christ first struck him down to the ground and blinded him at noontime with the "light from heaven." What a humiliation for a proud, cocky, self-righteous young man! But that was to shock him into attention. Now attentive, he heard a voice say to him, "Saul, Saul, why dost thou persecute me?" The reproach increased Saul's curiosity. "Who art thou, Lord?" It

NICHOLAS LLANES ROSAL, STD, PHL, MSJ

was a sheepish, humble voice acknowledging authority. To remove any doubt in Saul's mind, Jesus revealed Himself unequivocally: "I am Jesus whom thou art persecuting." Enlightened by the self-revelation, Saul realized that only moments ago, he was on his journey to round up Christ Himself—living in the soul and body of every Christian man and woman—to bring Him in chains to the synagogue. Then, "trembling and amazed, he said, 'Lord, what wilt thou have me do?'" It was the cry of a vanquished, contrite man who, begging for the Conqueror's own help, was ready to make amends. The Lord said to him, "Arise and go into the city and it will be told thee what thou must do" (Acts 9:2-19). Brought to Damascus by the men who journeyed with him, he neither ate nor drank for three days—a self-imposed penance to help drive any evil spirit away from him. Visited and helped by Ananias, he received instruction and was baptized. A new man, Saul became Christ's "chosen vessel" who carried his master's name among nations and kings and the children of Israel (Acts 9:1-19). Like St. Peter, he died a martyr in Rome—during Nero's persecutions—for the sake of the same Jesus whom he would have chained and brought into the synagogue.

Angels and Devils: Can They Make Miracles?

Jesus' miracles gave notice that, as the Son of God, He had the power over sickness, health, death, sin and sinners, the forces of nature, and even evil spirits. "For with authority and power, he commands the unclean spirits, and they come out" (Lk 4:26). St. Mark testifies, "And he cured who were afflicted with various diseases, and cast out many devils" (1:34). "And the unclean spirits, whenever they beheld him, fell down before him and cried out saying, 'Thou art the Son of God'" (3:11-12). Jesus Himself said He came *to cast out devils* (Mk 1:38-39). St. Luke describes how He cast out a legion of devils who had possessed a man. "When he saw Jesus, he fell down before him and crying out with a loud voice said, 'What have I to do with thee, Jesus, Son of the most High

God? I adjure thee by God, do not torment me!' And he asked him, 'What is thy name?' And he said to him, 'My name is Legion, for we are many.' And he entreated him earnestly not to drive them out of the country . . . "but to enter into the two thousand feeding swine." And the unclean spirits came out and entered into the swine . . . and the herd rushed down with great violence into the sea, and were drowned" (Mk 5:6-13). Hearing what had happened, people began to be afraid. "All the people of the Gerasene district besought him to depart from them; for they were seized with great fear" (Lk 8:37). "But the man who was healed, wanting to stay with Jesus, was told to go home to his relatives and to tell them all that the Lord had done for him and how he had shown mercy on him . . . And all marveled" (Mk 5:20).

Devils are known to have performed wonders. These are not miracles. Like angels that they are, St. Thomas Aquinas tells us that they can use and manipulate the forces embedded in nature—in particular, nature's capabilities unknown to eyewitnesses. They appear to perform miracles, because their knowledge and power exceed those of humans (1 q 114, art 4). They can change images in a man's mind; they can use light and air to make images. Devils, using their power to manipulate or control the forces found in men's bodies or spirits, can actually possess people as the gospels tell us. In a possession, the devil cannot replace the soul of a human being. But he can enter the senses, such as the hearing to make people hear what he wants them to hear. The wonders they make, according to St. Thomas, are ineffective, useless, and don't last. They delude (1 q 114, 4). Enemies of God, they cannot make wonders that glorify God or contribute to man's salvation. Hence, their marvels are not miracles.

St. Thomas observes that magicians can also make use of hidden forces found in nature. They can trick or play on the senses, especially vision, to create illusions—making things appear real when they are not. In some cases, a magician could contract with the devil. Recall Simon Magus who practiced sorcery (described in St. Paul [Acts 13:10] as "full of all guile and of all deceit, son of the devil"); seeing how the disciples who received the gifts of the

Holy Spirit performed wonders, Simon offered to pay St. Peter for those gifts. (Simony, a sin involving buying or selling sacred powers, originated from this incident told in Acts 8:19.)

God uses angels as instruments to perform miracles. On their own, they cannot make miracles, but they can do wonders, for God clothed them with supernatural powers. They can appear as humans (as in Old Testament times and at Jesus' resurrection), even as winds and flames of fires (Heb 1:6). Acting on their intercessory powers, they can, however, ask God to let them do miracles on behalf of humans. Angels have an important role in God's plan of salvation. It was an angel who was sent to Mary to announce she would be the mother of the Son of God. An angel appeared to Zachary to tell him of the birth of John the Baptist. Angels announced the birth of Jesus to the shepherds; Joseph was warned by an angel about Herod's intent to kill infant Jesus. An angel consoled Jesus in Gethsemane; angels announced to the women Jesus' resurrection. And angels will be there at the Last Judgment; but before then, they will be by every man and woman's side every day "to light and guard, to rule and guide" them.

To perform miracles, Jesus used simple, small, and large things in creation. He used water, bread, wind, fire, soil, and even spittle and the hem of His cloak. He used His eyes to glance, and a conversion followed. He used His voice to make known that He had forgiven sins; He used it to command dead people back to life and to calm the winds and the raging waters. He raised His hands to bless—to lay them on the heads of children, on the sick, and on the possessed. He took the hand of a dead child and gave her back to her father alive. He made miracles in the desert and the sea, inside and outside the temple, in homes and on the streets, on hills and mountains, and in the bodies and souls of people. He read the hatred and malicious intent in the hearts of Pharisees but put knowledge in the minds of His apostles. *To teach,* He used the people's surroundings as props: fields of wheat and fig trees; animals like the sheep, the lion, the scorpion, and even the snake; the elements, the weather, and the skies—anything that could bring faith to the hearts and minds of the multitudes and everything that could make them receive Him as the Son of God sent by the Father for their own sake.

Miracles and the Son of God

We have seen that miracles are God's mediums to communicate what men need to know to be saved. This is an essential element in a miracle. True miracles are salvation-ordained. They benefit those in whom the miracle takes place (as a blind man where the sight is restored) and in others who receive and respond to the message communicated through the miracle. A leper was cured by Jesus and was told to tell no one of his cure, but "so much the more, the tidings spread," bringing *great crowds together to hear Him* and to be cured of their sicknesses" (Lk 5:12-16; Jn 4:53; Mk 15:39; Mt 8:15).

When John the Baptist sent his disciples to ask Jesus if He was the "one to come," Jesus answered by describing what the Messiah was foretold to be doing: the blind see, the deaf hear, the dead rise, and the poor have the gospel preached to them (Lk 7:18-23). With those words, Jesus revealed Himself to be the Emmanuel prophesied by Isaiah (7:12-15)—the "God with us" who identified Himself with the poor, the "son of Man" who took up their infirmities and bore the burden of their ills (Mt 8:17). He chose not to be the king who was awaited by the Jews to reestablish and expand David's kingdom to the ends of the earth. Indeed, He was king but not of this earth (Jn 18:36). The five thousand whom He had fed in the desert wanted to proclaim Him king, but He fled to His mountain solitude (Jn 6:15). Even when He knew that the masses would be singing and shouting hosannas to Him upon entering Jerusalem, He would rather ride not on a chariot but on an ass, a poor man's transport. Refusing to accept the multitude's offer of a worldly crown, He had rather Himself be called Son of Man, a weak, helpless mortal who had nowhere to lay His head (Pss 11:4, 14:2; Eccl 1:13). In the beginning, He came down clothed in humanity; but in the end, He will come in the clouds in divinity's royal robes

(Mk 13:26) then sit at the right hand of the Father (Mk 14:62) to judge the living and the dead.

Compassion characterized the Son of Man's many miracles. In the desert where four thousand people had no food to eat, "Jesus called together his disciples and said, *'I have compassion on this crowd,* for they have nothing to eat; and I am unwilling to send them away fasting, lest they faint on the way.'" From seven loaves and "a few little fishes" that He multiplied, Jesus fed them (Mt 15:32-35). Now, when He went to a town called Naim, He saw a widow weeping as a dead man, her only son, was being carried out. *"And the Lord had compassion on her,* and said to her, 'Do not weep.' And he went up and touched the stretcher, and said, 'Young man, I say to thee, arise.' And he who was dead, sat up, and began to speak. And he gave him to his mother" (Lk 7:11-15). And there were two blind men who followed Him, crying out, *"Have pity on us, Son of David!"* "And Jesus said to them, 'Do you believe that I can do this to you?' They said, 'Yes, Lord.' Then he touched their eyes, saying, 'Let it be done to you according to your faith.' And their eyes opened" (Mt 9:27-30). Even when the crowd laughed at Him to scorn, Jesus, *in compassion for Jairus,* a Roman official, went into the room and took the official's dead daughter "by the hand, and the girl arose. And the report of this spread throughout all that district" (Mt 9:24-26).

Of all the miracles written in the gospels, St. John's narrative on the raising of Lazarus from the dead is the only one that tells of Jesus as "groaning in spirit" and "weeping," prompting the Jews to say, "See how he loved him" (Jn 11:35). It is one of the stories where Jesus is reported as spelling out clearly to His disciples and other eyewitnesses why He was going to perform a miracle. Told by Martha and Mary that Lazarus, whom he loved, was sick, Jesus told them, "This sickness is not unto death but **for the glory of God, that through it, the Son of God may be glorified**" (Jn 11:4). Four days later, Jesus finally was on His way to Bethany where Martha, facing Him, complained, "'Lord, if thou hadst been here, my brother would not have died. But even now, I know that whatever thou shalt ask of God, God will give it to thee.' Jesus said to her,

'Thy brother shall rise.' Martha said to him, 'I know that he will rise at the resurrection, on the last day.' Jesus said to her, **'I am the resurrection and the life.** He who believes in me, even if he dies, shall live; and whoever lives and believes in me, shall never die. Dost thou believe this?' She said to him, 'Yes, Lord, I believe thou art the Christ, the Son of God, who hast come into the world.'"

Accompanied by the women and His disciples and followed by a large crowd of Jews and many others, Jesus came to the tomb, a cave against which was laid a stone. Jesus said, "Take away the stone." Martha said, "Lord, by this time, he is already decayed, for he is dead four days." Jesus said to her, "Have I not told thee that if thou believe, thou shalt behold the glory of God?" They, therefore, removed the stone. And Jesus, raising His eyes, said, "Father, I give thee thanks that thou hast heard me. Yet, I knew that thou always hearest me, but *because of the people who stand round, **I spoke that they may believe that thou hast sent me.**" When He had said this, He cried out with a loud voice, **"Lazarus, come forth!" And at once, he who had been dead came forth"** (Jn 11:1-46).

Jesus performed this miracle on account of the people who stood around needing to be saved: His *apostles,* who, until before the resurrection, had not yet believed everything they had heard (Lk 24:6; Mt 27:65); His other followers, including *Martha and Mary,* whose faith needed to grow; the *Jews,* many of whom had seen His miracles but did not believe; and *the curious,* among them the Sadducees, who did not believe in resurrection. But above all, by raising Lazarus to life, Jesus wanted them to believe that *He was the Son of God whom the Father had sent.* **"For this is the will of my Father who sent me, that whoever beholds the Son, and believes in him, shall have everlasting life, and I will raise him up on the last day"** (Jn 6:39-40).

(Reflection: Six days before the Passover, Jesus and His disciples went to Bethany, where Mary and Martha made them supper. And Lazarus, who had been raised to life, was among those who were reclining at the table [Jn 12:2]. Lazarus' presence here *alive* was, among several other proofs, one powerful, undeniable evidence of the reality of Jesus' miracle. But how ecstatic a reunion that must have been! What kind of conversation must have taken place! What must have they talked about? That joyous reunion tells us how happy Jesus must be when, at His Eucharistic table, He meets one who was dead in sin but came back to life through the sacrament of penance and now "reclining" with others at the table of the Lord. Remember the parable of the lost sheep? With Him rejoicing must be choirs of angels and saints from heaven. Surely, Jesus would whisper love to the resuscitated soul, who should feel privileged to chat with Him, adore Him, and thank Him. An extraordinary, loving reunion for sure.)

Believers' and Unbelievers' Rewards

Many of the Jews who had come to Mary and had seen the raising of Lazarus believed in Him. But some of them went away to the Pharisees, who had been plotting against Him. They said, "What are we doing? For this man is working many signs. If we let him alone as he is, all will believe in him, and the Romans will come and take away both our place and our nation" (Jn 6:47-48). Satanic: Jesus' miracles evoke anger, jealousy, and feelings of hate?

They saw the signs—the miracles that struck awe among the multitude—but they did not accept the message: Christ was sent by the Father. On another occasion, Jesus had said to the same group of unbelievers, "I am from above. You are of this world. Therefore, if you do not believe that I am he, *you will die in your sins*" (Jn 24). St. Mark was emphatic: "He who does not believe shall be condemned" (16:16). Many unbelievers even accused Him of casting out devils by Beelzebub, the prince of devils (Lk 11:15). To these, He made clear He would have nothing to do with them; He would cast them away (Lk 11:23). When whole towns rejected Him, Jesus said, "Woe to thee, Corozain! Woe to thee, Bethsaida! For if Tyre and Sidon had been worked the miracles that have been worked in you, they would have repented long ago, sitting in sackcloth and ashes. But it will be more tolerable for Tyre and Sidon at the judgment than for you. And thou, **Capharnaum,** shall thou be exalted to heaven? **Thou shalt be thrust down to hell"** (Lk 10:13-16).

Recall how Jesus wept over Jerusalem, city of scribes and Pharisees who had rejected Him: "If thou hadst known, in this thy day, even thou, the things that are for thy peace! But now they are hidden from thy eyes. For days will come upon thee when thy enemies will throw up a rampart about thee, and surround thee and shut thee in on every site, and will dash thee to the ground and thy children within thee, and will not leave in thee one stone upon another, because thou hast not known the time of thy visitation" (Lk 19:41-44). Jesus visited Jerusalem, taught in the temple, preached to the mighty Pharisees, and performed miracles in their sight. In return, they plotted against Him. In the end, they nailed Him to a cross.

He warned those who had accepted His teachings to persevere: "Take heed how you hear; for to him who has, shall be given; and from him who does not have, even what he thinks he has, shall be taken away" (Lk 8:18). He condemned the false motive for seeking miracles. He said, "Amen, amen, I say to you. You seek me, not because you have seen signs, but because you have eaten of the loaves and have been filled" (Jn 6:26). Jesus made miracles for the sick, the possessed, and the blind out of the infinite goodness of His heart. But does He expect gratitude? Recall what Jesus told the leper who returned to Him after he realized he had been made clean: "Were not the ten made clean? But where are the nine? Has no one been found to return and give glory to God except this foreigner? And He said to him, 'Arise. Go thy way, for thy faith has saved thee'" (Lk 17:17-19).

To those who believed in Him, He promised great rewards: blessings, the gift of miracles and more miracles, and eternal life. He said to Thomas, *"Blessed* are they who have not seen, and yet have believed" (Jn 20:29). And He told His disciples, "These signs shall attend those who believe in my name: they shall cast out devils; they shall speak new tongues; they shall take up serpents, and if they drink any deadly thing, it shall not hurt them. They shall lay hands upon the sick and they shall get well" (Mk 16:17-18). And

NICHOLAS LLANES ROSAL, STD, PHL, MSJ

to those who have accepted His teachings and *shared* them with others like the seventy-two disciples who were sent forth to reap the harvest, they "will tread the might of the enemy, and nothing will hurt them." Their faith in Jesus brings them the gift of miracles. But more than that, they will rejoice exceedingly, for their "**names are written in heaven**" (Lk 10:19-20). As Jesus told Martha, "He who believes in me, even if he dies, shall live" (Jn 11:25). And to His apostles, He said, "You are they who have continued with me in my trials. And I appoint to you a kingdom, even as my Father has appointed to me, that you may eat and drink at my table in my kingdom; and **you shall sit upon thrones, judging the twelve tribes of Israel**" (Lk 22:28-30).

The Resurrection: Ultimate Miracle, Ultimate Meaning

No one can grant life on this earth and promise eternal life unless He is God. By His life, preaching, and miracles, Jesus proved His divinity. The multitudes adored Him; the devils acknowledged Him as the Son of God but plotted against Him (Mt 12:28; Jn 12:31). He performed miracles at will (Lk 4:30, 5:12-14). Even inanimate creatures—like the winds, the seas, water, and bread—obeyed Him (Lk 8:22-25). He was the Lord of the Sabbath, and His miracles testified to it (Mk 2:28, 3:1-16; Lk 6:6-11). By miracles, He proved He had the power to forgive sins (Mk 2:5-7; Lk 5:24). He was revealed by the Father as the Word (Jn 1:1-12) and the Beloved Son (Mt 1:17) who shared in the Father's power (Mk 13:26; Mt 16:27). He spoke with authority on divine law (Mk 10:1-12; Mt 5:17-48, 7:28) and revealed He would be the judge of all men at the end of time (Mk 13:26). By the psalms and the testimony of St. John (1 Jn 4:2) and St. Paul (Col 1:16), *He preexisted the world.* Having the power to read the thoughts of men, especially those of the Pharisees, He revealed the thoughts of Judas Iscariot: "Behold, the hand of him who betrays me is with me on the table. For the Son of Man indeed goes this way, as it has been determined" (Lk 22:21-22). And after the resurrection,

He would send the Holy Spirit (Mk 2:33). Knowing the future, He prophesied His death and resurrection (Mk 8:31; Mt 27:63; Lk 24:6). But *of all the miracles Jesus performed, it was His resurrection that most clearly proved His divinity.* It confirmed His credibility as the Son of God sent by the Father. It confirmed the faith of His followers, especially His apostles. It validated His miracles and teachings. Included in the Creed as an article of faith, the resurrection was the miracle of miracles. *Together with His passion and death, the resurrection has brought salvation to the world—its ultimate meaning.*

Death is the separation of the soul from the body; resurrection is the return of the life-giving soul to the body. By itself, the body is passive; without the soul, it is incapable of motion. Although a spirit, the soul, despite its immortality, is incapable of returning to the body by itself. By its very nature as a human soul, it is not endowed with the same power as that of the angels; but even with the supernatural power of an angel, the human soul, solely on its own, would be incapable of returning to the body to which it is, by nature, ordained. In the resurrection of Jesus, the soul was reunited to the body by divine power—the power of the Father, the Son, and the Holy Spirit—in His soul (Acts 2:32; See *Summa* 3, q 55, 4). *The return of Jesus' soul to His lifeless body through the divine power took place beyond the soul's natural capability, thereby making the reunion of His body and soul a miracle.* It happened in man's time—in history! It was an extraordinary event that happened *beyond* what was expected of nature.

But what is the meaning of this miracle? The answer to that question constitutes the cornerstone of our Christian faith. St. Paul polemically, but nonetheless forcefully, states the answer: "NOW, IF Christ is preached as risen from the dead, how do some among you say that there is no resurrection of the dead? But if there is no resurrection of the dead, neither has Christ risen; **and if Christ has not risen, vain then is our preaching, vain is your faith.** Yes, and we are found witnesses as to God, in that we have borne against God that he raised Christ—whom he did not raise. **For if Christ has not risen, vain is your faith, for you are still in your** sins" (1 Cor 15:12-17). Through Christ's resurrection, we became believers as St. Peter says, "Through him, you are believers in God who raised him up from the dead and gave him glory, so that your faith and hope might be in God" (1 Pt 1:21). It fulfilled Christ's prophecies: He would die and rise on the third day (Mk 8:31).

St. Thomas Aquinas gives five reasons why Christ rose from the dead:

1. *To manifest God's justice,* in accordance to Mary's canticle: *"He has put down the mighty from their thrones, and has exalted the lowly"* (Lk 1:52). As Son of Man, appearing as a weak and feeble human, abused and tortured, humiliated, and nailed to the cross, He was rewarded by the Father with the glorious resurrection.

2. *To kindle and confirm our faith,* according to St. Paul: "For though he was crucified through weakness, yet he lives through the power of God" (2 Cor 13:4).

3. *To raise our hope.* As we see Jesus, our head, rise from the dead, so we hope that we too shall rise. As St. Paul says, "If Christ is preached as risen from the dead, how do some among you say there is no resurrection of the dead?" (2 Cor 15:12).

4. *To renew the life of the faithful:* "For we were buried with him by means of baptism unto death, in order that, just as Christ has arisen from the dead through the glory of the Father, so we also may walk in newness of life" (Rom 6:4).

5. *To save us.* Christ was "delivered up for our sins, and rose again for our justification" (Rom 4:25).

By His resurrection, Christ gave us a pattern of man's own resurrection. His resurrection became an exemplary cause of our own as St. Thomas points out. His resurrection brought us grace (Jn 1:16) by which, primarily through baptism, we rise from sin and, secondarily, from the physical death from which we shall rise on the last day. And by His own voice, He shall raise the dead (Suppl. Q 76, 2).

After His resurrection, Jesus appeared to the eleven as they were at table and "upbraided them for their lack of faith and hardness of heart, in that they had not believed those who had seen him after he had risen" (Mk 16:14-15). But He appeared again and again to reassure them that He had truly risen. He continued to teach them, saying, "These are the words I spoke to you while I was yet with you . . . Then *He opened their minds that they might understand the Scriptures*" (Lk 24:45). Confirming their faith through miracles (Jn 21:1-14), He promised to send them the Holy Spirit to further instruct and strengthen them. In the end, they would all die a martyr's death for their faith, for the master they earlier had doubts about, for the Son of God who had been sent by the Father. He had founded His church on Peter the Rock; but now He charged him to be the shepherd of His flock—to feed His sheep with the same love he had professed to Jesus, to show compassion to the poor, to heal their sick, to forgive their sins, to preach, and to perform miracles in His name. And getting ready to ascend to heaven, He blessed them then commanded them, saying, "All power and on earth has been given to me. Go, therefore, and make disciples of all nations, baptizing them in the name of the Father, and of the Son, and of the Holy Spirit, teaching them to observe all that I have commanded you; and behold, I am with you all days, even unto the consummation of the world" (Mt 28:19-20). Then, the apostles and about five hundred people watched Him lift Himself up to the clouds and beyond—a divine miracle—from where He will come again to judge the living and the dead. Testifying to this miraculous ascent, two angels stood by them, saying to them, "Why do you stand looking up to heaven? This Jesus who has been taken up from you into heaven, shall come in the same way as you have seen him going up to heaven" (Acts 1:10-11).

From His ascension to the present to the end of time, Jesus has remained and will remain on earth in and through His mystical body—His church—preaching the gospel and performing miracles in His name through His saints.

(Reflection: Jesus truly rose from the dead. Many people saw Him. He appeared to Mary Magdalene, Mary, John, and Peter.

NICHOLAS LLANES ROSAL, STD, PHL, MSJ

At first, even His apostles doubted He had risen. Many others—including some who had witnessed Him ascend to heaven—remained unconvinced. We leave their fate in the hands of God. But we know that the centurion, the blind men, Martha, Mary, and countless others received the benefits of Christ's miracles because of their faith. By the power of faith, Jesus made the miracles work for the multitudes. Recall Jesus' words to those who received the kindness of a miracle: "Thy faith has saved thee" followed by "Go thy way and sin no more." Faith is an unmerited gift of God. To receive it, Christ wants us to prepare for it with good works performed out of humility and love. A humble heart is pleasing to God. It is the fertile ground where the seeds of faith can fall and live. Yet for faith to grow robust, we must strive to sin no more—Jesus' own words. Love is "sinning no more." Faith, lived by love, brings hope for what Jesus promised: eternal life. Amen.)

Christ's Miracles in the Gospels

F ROM ETERNITY, THE Creator *determined what everything in His creation can or cannot do.* His creation includes angels, who are pure spirits, and men, who are made of spirit and matter. He created the universe and everything in it: physical objects, time, movement, and any conceivable and inconceivable energy and potency embedded in them. The sum total of his creation and everything in it is what we come to know as *nature.* Nature is finite; it has limits. Only God is infinite; He is limitless. He can do what He wills to do—can *make any creature do what is beyond what He determined it can or cannot do.* And *that is what's called miracle.* But as the infinite goodness, He only does what is good for His creatures and, ultimately, for His glory as the Creator.

Christ's miracles reported by the Holy Spirit-inspired Evangelists do not only appear as evidence of God's power. They are proofs of Christ's love for believers and the rest of the world. But for those seeking to receive God's love through miracles, they must have an unwavering faith, humility to beg Christ's mercy and favor, and resignation to His will. Important to the effectiveness of the miracles is their willingness to accept the message the miracles convey, for miracles are God's way of communicating messages that man needs to know.

Because man lives in space and time that continually change, God makes miracles to happen in various places and different times to bring messages particular to his needs and circumstances. Loving God, ever knowing man's needs, looks after him everywhere and every moment of his time. Christ looked after the people in His time. He has continued and will continue to look after His church in various places in various times to the end of time. This is why the church over the centuries has witnessed countless miracles in various countries and in various eras to convey particular messages for the particular needs of the particular times. Although divine revelation (preceded by miracles) started from the first days of the Old Testament times and ended with the last of the apostles, miracles persisted in the world, particularly in the church, as *Christ's one continuing, extraordinary way* to *explain His teachings* through the centuries.

The Evangelists obviously could not determine the exact number of Christ's miracles. How could they have counted God's infinite mercies? His mercy is inexhaustible. Someone has put down seventeen as the number of Christ's miracles. That estimate is absolutely unrealistic in the face of the Evangelists' reports of *multitudes* gathering their sick and bringing them to Jesus. It would have been more especially impossible for them—presumably even by today's extensive media technology—to write about each of those miracles. John admits that even the miracles Christ did after the resurrection in the sight of the disciples "are not written in this [John's] book" (20:30). Then, he writes at the end of his gospel, "There are many other things that Jesus did, but if every one of these should be written, not even this world itself . . . could hold the books that would have to be written" (20:25). It's important to keep in mind that the miracles of Jesus were numberless because those show His limitless power. But it's more important to confess that He did not perform miracles for the sake of making them. They were by no means meant for people's amusement, not even for King Herod. They were God's mediums to attract people's curiosity and to gain their attention to His message. He made them for the meaning—His teaching—that He, through miracles, wanted them to know for their own sake—for their salvation. For every miracle is salvation-related.

All messages delivered through miracles are important and relevant. Their purpose is to light men's *minds* and, with that light, guide their *hearts*. Through miracles, the mind receives truth, which, as St. Thomas teaches, is perceived by the will as good. Good attracts; it prompts man to pursue it, attain it, and live it. Thus, God's truth delivered through miracles comes as *truth to be believed* and *truth to live by*. A true believer cannot separate the two: *faith and life go hand in hand*. Listen to what the Father said to Peter, James, and John during the transfiguration: "This is my beloved Son. <u>Hear Him</u>" (9:1-9). Believe that Jesus is the Father's beloved Son. Indeed! But obey Him too. Thus, for a man to reach heaven, it's not enough to say "I believe." He must live his faith. "If anyone loves me," Jesus said, "he will keep my word, and my Father will love him, and we will come to him and make our abode with him" (Jn 14:23-24).

Just as some miracles may be greater than others, depending on the potency they exceed, so may messages differ in importance, depending on their relatedness to the believers' salvation or on Christ's judgment itself. Washing the feet of Jesus with tears and anointing them with expensive oil to show sorrow for sin are more acceptable to Him than the monetary value of the oil (in those times, presumed imported from India) that could be given to the poor (Jn 12:3-8). Curing a man's withered hands on a Sabbath is more important than the ritual observance of the Sabbath (Mk 3:1-6). Indeed, believing Christ as the Son of God sent by the Father as an article of faith tops the belief (although important and relevant) in His power over devils and the winds and raging waters. Through Christ's miracles, Christian faith came to believe the basic revealed truths proclaimed in the Creed—the one God, the three divine persons, the incarnation, Christ's death and resurrection, etc. These are individual articles of faith that, *in the hierarchy of revealed truths,* top other important revelations necessary for salvation, including the sacraments. Although they appear as single articles of faith, these revealed truths—earth-shattering and all—are so *intimately interconnected* that they form one body, one belief, and one revelation to believe and profess. You believe in one God, Christ's crucifixion, etc., and you also believe in the sacraments. The revealed truths are fabrics so stitched together into one faith that not accepting one can result in unstitching others. To ensure that the "stitches" remain pure and strong, the Holy Spirit came down to brighten and confirm them even as Christ appointed Peter to look after them.

Most, if not all, of the revelations Jesus taught were preceded by miracles. As written by St. Matthew, even the beatitudes (5:3-22)—a cornerstone of the Christian way of life—were immediately preceded by many miracles: "And his fame spread into all Syria, and they brought to him all the sick suffering from various diseases and torments . . . and he cured them. And large crowds followed him from Galilee and Decapolis and Jerusalem and Judea and from beyond the Jordan" (4:23-25). After the miracles were done, He revealed the beatitudes, a way of life that creates peace among people—a foretaste of the eternal peace and happiness of those who believe and follow Him. But we must confess that Christ made one miracle—the resurrection, the one sign, the one most trustworthy testimony—that blanketed all His teachings. On that one miracle, as St. Paul (1 Cor 15:12-11) and St. Thomas Aquinas (3 q 53) teach, depends the trustworthiness of our faith. Together with the countless other miracles that speak of Christ's credibility, the resurrection builds a faith that is as indestructible as the rock on which He built His church.

Through miracles, Jesus, the master teacher, shows us a *way of life* to make us reach heaven. First, He catches man's attention with His awe-inspiring, curiosity-stimulating miracle to establish His authority and credibility. Then, attention achieved, Jesus delivers His message. When the message is accepted, man undertakes to fulfill it—with Jesus' own help. Fulfillment complete, man becomes one with the message-giver. The *process* realizes who and what Jesus is to us: *He is the way, the truth, and the life* (Jn 14:6). With His messages, *He is the Way* who leads us to the Father: "No one comes to the Father except through me" (Jn 4:6). With His revelations, *He is the Truth* to be believed: "You believe in God, believe also in me" (Jn 4:1). By instituting the sacrament of the Holy Eucharist, He gives us Himself—the "living bread" (Jn 6:33). "I am the living bread who came down from heaven. If anyone eat of this bread, he shall <u>live</u> forever, and the bread that I will give is my flesh for the life of the world" (Jn 6:51-52).

When put together, the messages conveyed by Jesus' miracles give us a way of life that leads us to our final destination—eternal happiness. The miracles, reported by the four evangelists, appear below with the messages they bear.

According to St. Matthew

1. Mary gives birth to Jesus while he respects His mother's virginity. *Reveals* God's predilection of Mary as pure and immaculate mother of His Son (1:18-25; Cf. essay 1). Let us love her too as our mother. Let's go to Mama Mary.
2. Stars guide Magi. *Reveals* that God uses nature to lead men to Christ (2:7-9). Let us use things of the earth, of creation, to reach Christ.
3. Angel warns Joseph in a dream to protect infant Jesus' life. *Reveals* Joseph's powerful role in the plan of mankind's salvation (2:19). Response: devotion to St. Joseph as Jesus' protector, our guide and defender. Let us go to Joseph!
4. Heals every sickness, torments in all Galilee, and the sick brought from Syria. *Reveals* that miracles bring people to God to glorify Him (4:23-24). Sickness may be God's way to bring man to Him. Let us be resigned to God's will.
5. Cures the sick in Decapolis, Jerusalem, and Judea. *Reveals* that miracles bring people to God to glorify Him (4:25). Sickness may be God's way to bring man to Him. God's will be done.
6. Touching a leper's hand, He cleanses him. *Reveals* that resignation to Christ's will pleases God (8:3). We ask God for favors not in our terms but in His.
7. Cures servant of centurion, who said he was not worthy that Jesus should enter his house. *Reveals* Jesus' admiration for humility, which serves as fertile ground for miracles and other divine favors (8:13). The more humble a man is, the more effective his prayer will be. The power of Jesus' miracles is not

NICHOLAS LLANES ROSAL, STD, PHL, MSJ

confined to space and time. Although Christ may at times feel distant to us, let us trust Him.

8. Cures Peter's mother-in-law; healed, she waits on Jesus and the apostles. *Reveals* Jesus' compassion for His followers' loved ones and gratitude expressed through service (8:14-15). The closer we are to Christ, the greater the favors He bestows on us.

9. Casts out spirits with one word and cures all the sick. *Reveals* power of faith (8:14). Let's have faith in Christ's word and promise.

10. Expels legion of devils in Gerasa from the possessed. *Reveals His* power over devils (8:8-24). However many and fierce the temptations around us, let's trust in God. (See essay 1.)

11. Cures Capharnaum paralytic on a pallet. *Reveals* His power to forgive sins (9:2-8). Before we ask for forgiveness, Christ already looks at us with compassion, ready to embrace us.

12. Raises Jairus' twelve-year-old daughter back to life. *Reveals* Jesus' compassion for parents; faith wins over unbelievers' derision (9:13-18). Let not obstacles to prayer and observance of virtue deter us from doing what faith and love urge us to do.

13. Woman touches Jesus' hem; hemorrhage is cured. *Reveals* that reverent fear and unyielding faith inspired by Christ's presence lead to healing miracles (9:20-23). Anything connected with Jesus—however small it appears to human eyes—becomes a conduit of His great mercy and power.

14. Two blind men follow Jesus, publicly confessing unwavering faith in Jesus' power amid unsympathetic people, and receive their sight back. *Reveals* power of faith (9:27-31). Let's glorify God even in the midst of opposition.

15. Drives devil from dumb demoniac. *Reveals* Christ's power over devils. *"Never has the like been seen in Israel"* (9:32-34). We should never underestimate the power of devils, but we should never fail to trust the infinite power of Christ either. Let us not despair in the face of fierce temptations.

16. Restores withered hand to health on a Sabbath. *Reveals* His power over the Sabbath (12:9-14). Christ will show greater love for us, especially when we are in the midst of fierce spiritual trials. Let's keep up our faith in Him.

17. Prophesies His resurrection. *Reveals* His all-knowing power and His authority to lay down His life at will and the power to take it back again (12:40-42). Man's life is in God's hands. Let's be resigned to His will.

18. Feeds the five thousand. *Reveals* His compassion over the multitude and power over such inanimate things as bread and prepared fish. Refuses a self-serving adulation that offers a worldly crown. Wrong motive for seeking Him (14:13-21). Let's cleanse our motive as we perform works of charity, but let our prayer be trusting in His divine mercy, which exceeds our expectations.

19. Walks on water. *Reveals* His divine power over creation (14:22-33). We too can tread on the waters of trials and temptations if our faith in God is unwavering and our love of neighbor is sincere.

20. At Genesar, as soon as they recognized him, they spread the news, and they brought to Him *all the sick,* entreating Him to let them *touch* but the *tassel of His cloak.* And all who touched it were saved" (14:36-). *Reveals* that anything connected to Him is a conduit of His miraculous power—a basis for veneration of saints' relics—in accordance to St. John's "Of his fullness we have all received" (1:16).

21. On the mountain along the sea of Galilee, "great crowds came to him, bringing with them the dumb, the blind, the lame, the maimed, and many others, and they set them at his feet, and he cured them . . . And they glorified the God of Israel" (15:29-31). *Reveals* His inspiring power on people to glorify God. Let's make mental pilgrimages as often as we can to invoke Christ's healing power.

22. Feeds four thousand (15:32-34). *Reveals* His compassion for the poor and the hungry. People who follow Him will not be abandoned in their needs. His compassion exceeds your needs.

23. Jesus transfigures (17:1-8). *Reveals* His glorified body; His fellowship with Moses and Elias, who had prophesied His coming; His passion, death, and resurrection; and the role of angels as Jesus' consolers in His agony. Meditate on the

meaning of life—the eternal purpose of our souls—and accept whatever God's will is for us. Let's look forward to a glorious end in God's eternal paradise.

24. Drives devil out of a father's young son, whom Jesus' disciples could not help. *Reveals* His compassion and stresses to His disciples the need for a strong faith: "If you have faith like a mustard seed, you will say to this mountain, 'Remove from here'; and it will remove. And nothing will be impossible to you. <u>But this kind can be cast only by prayer and fasting</u>." The young man was "a lunatic and suffers severely." This tells us of degrees of Satanic possession and calls for intense penance, including fasting, and sincere prayer. Implies disciples' inadequate preparation. (A message to ministers before administering the sacrament of penance.)

25. Restores sight to two blind men in Jericho. They follow Him. *Reveals* Jesus' compassion. Miracles induce people to follow Christ. We can try to repay God's favors by following Him to Calvary through prayer and penance. But we will never totally repay everything God has done for us. Yet try we must.

26. Prophesies where colt could be found and brought to Him to ride on His entrance into Jerusalem (21:2-5). *Reveals* His humility and omniscient power. His transport is a colt, not a chariot. God knows when and where we are every moment of our lives. Let's keep our thoughts, our motives, and our actions in line with His commands.

27. Foretells destruction of Jerusalem (24:1-2). *Reveals* omniscience and need for watchfulness. Every man has his hour of trial. Let's be prepared!

28. Peter weeps bitterly (26:75). *Reveals* conversion prompted by Christ's compassion. No man can rely on himself. Without God, man is nothing—easily can he fall into sin! But like Peter, let him be sincere in his repentance with Jesus' own help.

29. Temple curtain is rent from top to bottom, sun darkens, earth shakes, and the dead appear on the streets of Jerusalem (27:53, 27:75). *Reveals* that even nature protests against Jesus' death; a pagan centurion proclaims Christ's innocence aloud and

confesses Jesus to be the Son of God. We too must make that confession as often as we can.

30. The resurrection (28:1-16). *Reveals* Christ's divinity, divine justice, validation of His teachings and our faith, opening of the gates of heaven, graces gained for baptism, resurrection of the just, triumph over death, increase of hope to see God face-to-face, and the church becoming the New Jerusalem. (See essay 1.)

According to St. Mark

31. Cures a demoniac (1:23-27). *Reveals* Christ's power over demons. The miracle elicits a devil's confession of Him as the Holy One of God and gains attention all around. Let's ask Christ to drive away the demons in us so that we can belong to Him and Him alone.

32. Cures Peter's mother-in-law. *Reveals* that miracles increase devotion to God. He cares about apostles' relatives. Gratitude, expected of miracle beneficiaries, is expressed through service (See Mt 8:14-15). We thank God by doing good for others.

33. "The whole town had gathered together at the door. And he cured many who were afflicted with various diseases, and cast out many devils" (1:29-31). *Reveals* Christ's compassion for all and shows His divine power over sickness and health and over devils. We always ask Christ's power to heal our weaknesses, our compulsions, and our vices.

34. Cures leper (1:40-45). *Reveals* that humility and resignation to the will of God prompt miraculous cure. Respect for the Mosaic purification law ("go show yourself to the high priest")—an allegorical picture of the sacrament of penance. Let's always be thankful to God for daily favors, responding to His call for adoration every moment of our lives as much as we can.

35. Cures paralytic in Capharnaum (2:1-12). *Reveals* Christ's power to forgive sins. We have all been paralyzed by sin in one way or another. Let's hope in God's healing power and forgiveness of our sins.

NICHOLAS LLANES ROSAL, STD, PHL, MSJ

36. Cures man's withered hands (3:1-6). *Reveals* His power over Sabbath. Shows Pharisees' deceitfulness. Trust in God's compassion. Let's beware of our own hypocrisy; pray for and avoid people with hypocritical motives.

37. "For he healed many so that as many as had ailments were pressing upon him to touch him" (3:9-10). *Reveals* how closeness to Jesus brings miraculous power to bear. Let's become closer to Jesus through prayer and good works and hope for God's forgiveness for our sins.

38. Calms the storm at sea (4:35-38). *Reveals* His power over forces of nature. We ask Christ to calm our propensity to sin and our feelings of anger, hate, and revenge. But let's do our part.

39. Expels devils in Gerasa (5:1-15). *Reveals* His power over devils. Commands healed man to glorify God and publish God's mercies. Acknowledge God's works in and for you, but show your gratitude to Him through love of neighbor.

40. Raises daughter of Jairus, one of the rulers of the synagogue, back to life. (5, 2:35-43). *Reveals* Christ's special compassion for Jairus, in particular, and parents, in general. We must do good even in the face of opposition and ridicule. Let's avoid being annoyed by the term *do-gooder* when used against us for doing a sincerely charitable act of love for a neighbor.

41. Cures woman from twelve-year hemorrhaging (5:24-30). *Reveals* faith to obtain Christ's mercy and miracle cure. "Daughter, thy faith has saved thee. Go in peace, and be thou healed of thy affliction." Let us always have that faith in God as we pray for temporal favors but especially for the forgiveness of our sins.

42. Cures the possessed daughter of a gentile Canaanite woman (7:24-30). *Reveals* that miracle works on everyone having confidence in Christ, regardless of ethnicity, citizenship, and residence. God's miracles are no respecter of people. God loves everyone, including those whom people consider beneath them.

43. Makes a deaf-mute in Decapolis hear and speak. *"Taking him aside from the crowd,* He put his fingers into the man's ears, and spitting, He touched the man's tongue. And looking up

to heaven, He sighed and said to him, 'Ephpheta,' that is 'Be opened.' And his ears were at once opened, and the bond of his tongue was loosened, and he began to speak correctly" (7:31-28). *Reveals* how Jesus, taking the man aside from the crowd, wants, at times, to be alone with people as on a heart-to-heart dialogue. (A model for spiritual retreat.) Also reveals how He can make use of things in and around Him, such as spittle, to perform miracles. Let's commune with God—thinking of His presence everywhere. Let's set aside time just to talk to Him.

44. Multiplies seven loaves and a few little fishes to feed the four thousand who had been with Him three days. After the multitude "ate and were filled," the disciples filled seven baskets with the remnants (8:1-9). *Reveals* His divine power, compassion, and generous mercy that surpass—by symbolic *seven baskets of leftovers!*—our needs, our weaknesses, and our sins. Symbolizes the seven sacraments.

45. Cures a blind man at Bethsaida. First, He applies spittle to his eyes then touches them (8:22-25). *Reveals* how a miracle, based on man's total confidence in God's will, may, in His divine plan, happen in steps but will surely occur. Implies full trust in God and need *for patient* and *persevering prayer.* We shouldn't despair when our prayers aren't answered immediately when we need it. God has a better plan than ours.

46. Foretells His passion, death, and resurrection (8:21-33). *Reveals* His divine power to lay down and bring back His life *at will.* We are all in the hands of God. Let's resign to His will.

47. Jesus is transfigured with Elias and Moses present (9:1-9). *Reveals* the harmony of the Old Testament revelations and the teachings of Jesus. Also revealed is the glorified Jesus. Peter writes, "We saw his glory" (2 Pet 1:16). The radiance of His clothing proceeds from the glory of his divine person. Things connected with Jesus become conduits of His power, mercy, and glory. The Father's voice "out of the cloud" proclaims Jesus once again as He did during His baptism, "This is my beloved Son," but further commands obedience to Him and His teachings, "This is

my beloved Son. Hear him." Faith and life go hand in hand. It's not enough to say "I believe" to be saved. We must live our faith.

48. Jesus, out of compassion, drives the devil from a young boy possessed from infancy. "Often times, the devil would throw him into the fire and into the waters to destroy him," the boy's father told Jesus. Listening to his plea, Jesus said, "'If you can believe, all things are possible to him who believes.' At once the father cried out and said in tears, 'I do believe.'" But he might not have believed enough, so he asked Jesus, "Help my unbelief." Jesus then commanded the devil to leave the boy and "enter him no more." "Crying out and violently convulsing the boy, the devil went out, leaving him for dead. But Jesus took the boy by the hand, raised him, and he stood up" (9:13-28). Later, His disciples asked Him privately why they could not expel the devil. *Jesus reveals* to them, "This kind can be cast out in no way except by prayer and fasting." His response showed the disciples' inadequate preparation, if any, for the critical task of driving the demon. Herein is revealed an essential requirement of anyone attempting to exorcise. (*An important notice to priests' preparation before administering the sacraments of penance and anointing of the sick.*) Prayer and penance ward off temptation.

49. Restores sight to Bartimeus, a blind beggar, whom the crowd wanted to stop from incessantly crying out, "Jesus, Son of David, have mercy on me!" Talking to the blind man who had been brought in His presence, Jesus asked him, "What shouldst thou have me do for thee?" Bartimeus replied, "'Rabboni, that I may see.' Jesus said to him, 'Go thy way. Thy faith has saved thee.' At once, he received his sight, and followed him along the road" (10:46-52). *Reveals* Jesus' compassionate response to a *persistent, persevering plea* from an *unwavering faith* that inspires others to believe. Let's pray perseveringly if we expect God to listen to us.

50. Rides colt to enter Jerusalem (11:1-11). *Reveals* His humility and His character as Son of Man, who rides into the city not on a chariot but on a young beast of burden, a poor man's transport. Let's avoid excesses.

51. Curses a fig tree, which *instantly* withers (11:20-25). *Reveals* essential characteristics of effective prayer: faith, hope, and love. He says to the apostles, "Have *faith* in God. Amen I say to you: whoever says to this mountain, 'Arise, and hurl thyself into the sea,' and does not waver in his heart, but believes that whatever he says will be done, it shall be done for him. Therefore, I say to you, all things whatever you ask for in prayer, believe that you shall receive (*hope*), and they shall come to you. And when you stand up to pray, forgive whatever you have against anyone (*love*), that your Father in heaven forgive you your offenses." Let faith, hope, and love—all together—shine in our lives.

52. Foretells the destruction of Jerusalem, the end of time, and the universal judgment (13:1-37). *Reveals* His omniscience, His divine justice, His role as judge of the living and the dead, and His divine mercy that will shorten the days of "the abominations" for the sake of the "elect" and a warning to be watchful *for you do not know when the time is.* "But of that day or hour, *no one knows,* neither the angels in heaven nor the Son, but the Father only." With God's mercy, we try to be in the state of grace and be prepared any moment when He calls. Let's pray for perseverance—a special gift of God.

53. Instructs two disciples to go into the city and follow a man with a pitcher of water, whom they would inquire about his guest chamber for the Passover meal. "And the disciples went forth, and came into the city and found just as he had told them" (14:13-16). *Reveals* His omniscience and His divine right to use what God gave man to use and "own." We are only users and borrowers of God's creation and its fruits. Use them for others and for His glory.

54. Reads Judas Iscariot's mind (14:10, 17-21). *Reveals* His omniscience, His respect for man's freedom (He could have stopped Judas from carrying out his plot to betray Him), and His desire to fulfill the Father's will to save the world through His passion, death, and resurrection. With God's help, let's use our freedom for our own good and not for our self-destruction.

55. Foretells Peter's denial (14:26-31). *Reveals* His omniscience, His patience on well-meaning followers, and ultimately, His compassion and forgiveness on those who repent and "weep bitterly" over their sins. Let's always be aware of our weaknesses and not be presumptuous of our strength, which we don't have without Christ. (See essay 1.)

56. Miracles on Golgotha: darkness and centurion's profession of faith. "Truly, this man was the Son of God." In the temple: the curtain tore in two from top to bottom (16:33-37). *Reveals* His divine power over nature and love for everyone, including the centurion, a pagan, to whom He granted the grace of conversion. *Conversion happened as he was reflecting on Jesus' suffering on the cross* in the midst of nature's miraculous revolt over the injustice perpetrated on Him. We repent our sins that cause us to revolt against Christ. We pray for sinners.

57. The resurrection—See essay 1 and no. 30 above.

58. The ascension—See essay 1 and no. 30 above.

59. Reward of faith to believers: eternal salvation and gift of miracles (16:16-18). *Reveals* how believers "shall be saved" and how "signs" shall attend them: "In my name they shall cast out devils; they shall speak in new tongues; they shall take up serpents, and if they drink any deadly thing, it shall not hurt them; they shall lay hands upon the sick and they shall get well." We pray for a persevering faith that, with Jesus and the Holy Spirit, will carry us onto the Father at the end of our lives.

According to St. Luke

60. The Holy Spirit descends upon Jesus in bodily form as a dove while "a voice came from heaven," saying, "Thou art my beloved Son. In thee I am well pleased" (3:31-22). *Reveals* the Father's testimony that Jesus is *the* "Son of God" that had been foretold by the prophets. When the scribes and Pharisees would later ask Him to produce witnesses to validate His preaching and miracles, Jesus would bring in the Father as His witness.

Will Christ be on our side when we appear before the Father when we die? We pray. Amen.

61. Led by the Spirit about the desert for forty days without eating, Jesus was sought by the devil to be tempted to perform miracles. First, the devil wanted the hungry Jesus to command a stone to become a loaf of bread. Then, he led Jesus up to see all the kingdoms of the world "in a moment of time," telling Him he would give all that power and glory to Him if He would worship before him. Finally, the devil dared Jesus to throw Himself down from the pinnacle of the temple to prove He was the Son of God whom angels would come to save lest He dash His foot against a stone. *Reveals* Christ's teachings: "Not by bread alone shall man live but by every word of God," "The Lord thy God shalt thou worship, and him only shalt thou serve," and "Thou shalt not tempt the Lord thy God." This gospel story reveals the nature of the devil as an absolute liar claiming ownership of kingdoms and power he doesn't have. He makes totally deceitful promises to give what doesn't belong to him. Importantly, he shows here his unbroken pride—cause of his having been thrown out of heaven—that arrogates to himself the dignity and power of God. Note his eternal envy of the Son of God. The idea of making himself equal to God was the same thought he used to tempt Adam and Eve with to disobey the Creator: "No, you shall not die; for God knows that when you eat of it (forbidden tree), your eyes will be opened and you will be like God" (Gn 3:4-5). Beware of those critical moments of weakness. We pray to our Father that we may not be led into temptation (i.e., more than we can bear) but pray that He deliver us from evil. Amen.

62. After Jesus read Isaiah's prophecy about the prophet to come, He said to the Jews, "Today this Scripture has been fulfilled in your hearing." When the Jews heard that, they dragged Him to the brow of the hill that they might throw Him down headlong. "But he, passing through their midst, went his way" (4:29-30). *Reveals* His divine power. He foresees the persecution against Him that would end in His passion and

death. We pray that we be spared from Christ's enemies' evil intentions and machinations.

63. There was a man full of leprosy who besought Jesus, saying, "Lord, if thou wilt, thou canst make me clean." Stretching forth His arm, Jesus touched him, saying, "I will. Be thou made clean." And immediately the leprosy left him. Then, Jesus said, "Go, show thyself to the priest, and offer the gift for thy purification as Moses commanded" (5:12-14). *Reveals* that Jesus is moved by the beneficiary's humility, resignation, and simple faith when He hears *"if thou wilt."* In response, Jesus gives a decidedly firm "I will." He teaches us resignation as a critical element in our prayers (remember the Our Father?). After all, all miracles occur because God wills them; there are no accidental miracles. *Shows* us that favors are granted *in God's terms*, not always as we wish. Let's be resigned to God's wisdom and will always.

64. Cures a paralytic in Capharnaum (5:18-26). *Reveals* power to read thoughts and power to forgive sins. Man's paralysis implies the cause—sin. Shows that the miracle recipient must be clean before receiving Christ's favor. To obtain God's favors, it behooves us to have our minds and hearts as clean as can be.

65. Jews accuse Jesus of disobeying the law of the Sabbath. Proves His authority by the Holy Scripture and by His miracle (6:1-11). *Reveals* He is the Lord of the Sabbath. Seeing the disciples picking and eating ears of grain in the middle of a farm on a Sabbath, the Jews condemned Jesus for letting His disciples break the Sabbath law. Christ told them that if David and the hungry people with him could eat the temple loaves of proposition, then He, higher than David, would allow His hungry disciples to pick and eat ears of grain on the Sabbath. He is Lord of the Sabbath. Similarly, when, in the temple on a Sabbath, He saw a man with a withered hand (put there as a bait by the Pharisees) and Christ's enemies were watching if He would cure, Jesus asked them "if it is lawful on the Sabbath to do good, or to do evil? Or to save a life, or to destroy it?" Looking around upon them, He said to the man, "Stretch

forth thy hand," and his hand was restored. Miracles occur out of Christ's sheer goodness. When we feel crippled by circumstances of jobs, home responsibilities, and other worries, let's put our trust in the Lord who will not fail us.

66. Heals the servant of a centurion who sent Jewish elders to beseech Jesus to save his servant. The elders described the man to Jesus *as worthy* of Jesus' favor, a benefactor who had built them a synagogue. As Jesus and the elders were on their way to the house, the centurion sent friends to say to Him, "Lord, do not trouble thyself, for I am not worthy that thou shouldst come under my roof; that is why I did not think myself worthy to come to thee. But say the word and my servant will be healed. For I, too, am a man subject to authority and have soldiers subject to me. And I say to one, 'Go', and he goes . . . and to my servant, 'Do this,' and he does it." And when the messengers returned to the centurion's house, they found the servant in good health (7:1-10). *Reveals* Jesus' admiration for great humility and great faith.

(Reflection: Here was a respected, influential military-political leader yet considered himself unworthy to talk to Jesus face-to-face, his reason for sending a delegation of Jewish leaders and friends to talk to Him on his behalf. Too unworthy to see himself personally appearing to Jesus, he thought even more unworthy was his home where his servant at the point of death lay. A great lesson in faith and humility for all.)

67. In Naim, raising a young man back to life, He gave him to his widowed mother amid the crowd glorifying God and saying "A great prophet has risen among us" and "God has visited his people" (7:11-17). *Reveals* Christ's deep compassion and power over life and death. Even if we are dead in sin—God forbid—Christ's compassion will raise us up if we do our part: repent and make amends.

68. Awakened by His disciples from sleep in the boat that had taken in water, Jesus calms down the storm (8:22-25). *Reveals*

His divine power over elements but tells us that as long as He is with us, there's nothing to fear. We ask Him for perseverance.

69. Expels legion of devils in Gerasa (8:26-39). (See no. 39 above.)

70. Brings Jairus' daughter back to life (8:40-56). *Reveals* His compassion, power over life and death, and determination to do good despite opposition and ridicule.

71. Cures woman's hemorrhage (9:20-23). (See no. 13 above.)

72. Feeds five thousand in the desert (9:12-17). *Reveals* divine compassion. His generosity exceeds man's needs and expectations, allegorized in twelve baskets of remnants. Abundance, meant to be shared, provides opportunities to love others.

73. Jesus transfigures (9:28-36). (See no. 47 above.)

74. Casts out devil from dumb man. Pharisees accuse Him of casting out devil by Beelzebub (11:14-23). *Reveals* divine wisdom and power over Satan and followers. Condemning the Pharisees' blasphemy and explaining God's miraculous power, He said, "Every kingdom divided against itself is brought to desolation, and house will fall upon house. If, then, Satan also is divided against himself, how shall his kingdom stand? Because you say that I cast out devils by Beelzebub. Now, if I cast out devils by the finger of God, then the kingdom of God has come upon you." We pray that we remain on God's side every moment of our lives.

75. Cures stooped woman who, for eighteen years, had the sickness caused by Satan. "When Jesus saw her, he called her to him and said to her, 'Woman, thou art delivered from thy infirmity.' And He laid his hands upon her, and instantly she was made straight and glorified God." The synagogue owner condemned Jesus for the miracle because it was the Sabbath (13:10-16). *Reveals* Jesus' compassion. He has power over the Sabbath. Love of neighbor precedes blind observance of the Sabbath. Jesus explains, "Hypocrites! Does not each one of you on the Sabbath loosen his ox or ass from the manger, and lead it forth to water? And this woman, daughter of Abraham as she is, whom Satan has bound, lo, for eighteen years, ought not she to

be loosened from this bond on the Sabbath?" *Lord, unbind us from our sinful ways!*

76. On a Sabbath in the house of one of the rulers of the Pharisees, Jesus was invited to eat. There, He met a man who had an edema. Reading their thoughts, Jesus asked the lawyers and Pharisees, "Is it lawful to cure on the Sabbath?" But they remained silent. "And he took and healed him (*the plant*) and let him go. Then, He said to them, 'Who of you shall have an ass or an ox fall into a pit, and will not immediately draw him up on the Sabbath?" (14:1-8). *Reveals* His divine compassion and power over the Sabbath and shows Pharisees' evil intentions. *From evil minds, Lord, deliver us.*

77. Cures ten lepers. One returns to say thanks (17:11-19). *Reveals* Christ's compassion. He expects gratitude: "Were not ten made clean? Has no one been found to return and give glory to God except this foreigner (a Samaritan)?" Stresses importance of faith as an important element in obtaining a miracle. Teaches that the offering to a priest is testimony to leper's gratitude for the cure. Familiarity and ethnicity are no excuse for not acknowledging a good deed.

78. Cures blind man in Jericho (18:35-43). *Reveals* Christ's compassion. Stresses unwavering faith as a signal element in obtaining a miracle. (See no. 44 above.)

79. Disciples find a colt in the city where Jesus said it would be. He would ride it to enter Jerusalem amid a multitude singing hosannas on the road next to the Garden of Olives (Lk 19:29-31). *Reveals* Christ's all-knowing power and evokes response to Pharisees' angry demand for Jesus to rebuke His disciples: "I tell you that if these keep silence, the stones will cry out." Shows that Christ will not stop people from glorifying God despite the Pharisees' evil opposition and deep-seated envy. As believers, we should continue professing our faith even in the face of hatred, ridicule, and opposition.

80. As foretold by Jesus, disciples find and follow a man carrying a pitcher of water to where He and His apostles would celebrate the Passover (22:10-13). *Reveals* His omniscience and His right

as God to use, when it pleases Him, what men "possess." We acknowledge His almighty power as creator—as possessor or owner—of the entire universe and *everything* in it. We are borrowers of His earth.

81. Jesus institutes the Holy Eucharist. Performs an extraordinary miracle by turning bread into His body and wine into His blood (22:24-30). *Reveals* His divine power and His desire to unite Himself intimately with believers through the Holy Eucharist as testimony to His union with them in the next life—memorable evidence of His continuing presence in the world as He promised (Mt 28:20). Teaches that Jesus is the bread from heaven that gives eternal life, not as the bread the Israelites ate in the desert (Jn 6:22-23). Shows that Jesus gave the power to His disciples to change bread into His body and wine into His blood—a silent but awesome miracle performed daily by His priests—so that He would continue feeding His followers with the bread of heaven and giving them His blood to drink until the end of time. How can we not approach Him and ask Him to come visit with us as often as we can in Holy Communion? He is the pledge of our eternal happiness!

82. Restores the ear of a high priest's servant. When the apostles saw who were with Judas, they said to Him, "Lord, shall we strike with the sword?" And "one of them struck the servant of the high priest and cut off his right ear. But Jesus answered and said, 'Bear with them this far.' And He touched his ear and healed him" (22:49-52). *Reveals* His great mercy even on one among His enemies who were going to take Him away. Shows the need to control impulses, especially to hurt; forbear instead. Jesus says, "I have a better plan for them." We pray earnestly to our Father "to forgive us our trespasses as we forgive those who trespass against us."

83. Thief undergoes conversion—an internal miracle. He repents, acknowledges Jesus as Lord, and prays, "Lord, remember me when thou comest to thy kingdom." Jesus assures Him, "Amen, I say to thee, this day thou shalt be with me in paradise" (23:29-43). *Reveals* that repentance, faith, and humility greatly

appeal to Christ's mercy and power. Christ forgives no matter how sinfully a man has lived if he truly repents and has an unwavering faith in His mercy and power. *Lord, give us a happy death—with You in us—when the last moment comes. Amen.*

84. Darkness came over the whole land until the ninth hour, the sun darkened, and the curtain of the temple was torn in the middle. Extraordinary, awesome physical coincidences! (23:44-45). *Reveals* that even nature grieves over the unjust death of the Son of God. Let's grieve for our sins.

85. Jesus rises from the dead (24:1-7). (See essay 1 and no. 30 above.)

86. Jesus stands in the midst of the apostles in a closed-door room: "And while they were talking of these things, Jesus stood in their midst, and said to them, 'Peace to you! It is I, do not be afraid.' But they were startled and panic-stricken, and thought that they saw a spirit. And he said to them, 'Why are you disturbed, and why do doubts arise in your hearts? See my hands and feet, that it is I myself. Feel me and see, for a spirit does not have flesh and bones, as You see I have.' And having said this, he showed them his hands and his feet" (24:36-41). *Reveals His* divine power and victory over death. Vindicates His enemies. Validates His teachings and promises and reproves apostles' unbelief. We ask Jesus' forgiveness for our lack of faith. *"Lord, that we may see!"* (See essay 1 and no. 57 above.)

87. Jesus ascends to heaven. "Now he led them out towards Bethany, and he lifted up his hands and blessed them. And it came to pass as he blessed them, that he parted from them and was carried up into heaven. And they worshipped him, and returned to Jerusalem with great joy. And they were continually in the temple, praising and blessing God. Amen" (24:50-51). *Reveals* fulfillment of His promise to return to His Father as a reward for accomplishing the mission given Him. Shows the world the way to eternal happiness. We belong there—beyond the blue. *Lord, take us there where You live that we may glorify You forever with the angels and saints. Amen.* (See essay 1, no. 58, and no. 64 above.)

According to St. John

88. "And the Word was made flesh, and dwelt among us . . . The only-begotten Son, who is in the bosom of the Father, he has revealed him" (1:14-18*). Reveals* the divine and human nature of the Word who was incarnated in the womb of the Virgin Mary. *Lord, You became man to show us Your humility as a way to the Father. We believe that You came down to earth to redeem us from sin.* (See essay 1.)

89. Changes water into wine in Cana wedding (2:1-12). Reveals (a) Christ's divine power, (b) sacramental character and sacredness of marriage, (c) Mary's role as powerful intercessor, and (d) His first miracle that made His disciples accept Him. *Lord, that we may believe always in You!*

90. Discloses to a Samaritan woman her own secret life (4:1-45). Showing His omniscience, He *reveals Himself as the Messiah.* "The woman said to him, 'I know that Messiah is coming (who is also called Christ), and when he comes he will tell us all things.' Jesus said to her, **'I who speak to you am he.'''** He states why He was sent by the Father: "My food is to do the will of him who sent me, to accomplish his work." And "far more believed because of his word. And they said to the woman, 'We no longer believe because of what thou hast said, for we have heard for ourselves and we know that this is in truth the Savior of the World.'" The truthfulness of what one believes comes from the trustworthiness of the source of the subject to be believed. Who can top Christ's truthfulness and authority? "I am the way, the life, and the *truth,*" He said. May we also believe and do Christ's will every moment of our lives.

91. Performs second sign, coming from Judea into Galilee: cures the son of a royal official (4:46-54). *Reveals* His power over sickness and health. The miracle led the royal official and his whole household to believe. *Lord, give us the royal official's humility, his faith in your power and in you as the Messiah.* (See essay 1.)

92. Cures a man, lame for thirty-eight years, who had always missed the healing water of the pool (Bethsaida) immediately after it moved. Seeing him, Jesus said to him, "'Dost thou want to get well?' The sick man answered him, 'Sir, I have no one to put me into the pool when the water is stirred, for while I am going, another steps down before me.' Jesus said to him, 'Rise, take up thy pallet and walk.' And at once, the man took up his pallet and began to walk. Now that day was a Sabbath." Answering the Jews who told him he was not allowed to pick up the pallet, the man said, "He who made me walk told me to take it up. Afterwards, Jesus, finding him in the temple, said, 'Behold, thou art cured. Sin no more, lest something worse befall thee'" (5:5-13). *Reveals* Christ's divine power and compassion. Christ, in His wisdom and love, grants us favors without our asking, but His favors have to be repaid with persevering love. "Sin no more," He says. We pray for perseverance, a special gift from Christ.

The miracle stirred wrath among the Jews, who accused Him of not only breaking the Sabbath but also "making himself equal to God." To this, Jesus insisted that His work was His Father's. "For whatever he does, the Son also does in like manner. For the Father loves his Son, and shows him all that he himself does. And greater works than these he will show him that you may wonder." Among these wonders are raising the dead, not only to an earthly life, but also unto the "resurrection of judgment" where Jesus will appear with the "power to render judgment" on the good and the evil. *We believe in You, Lord, as the judge of the good and evil. May we be on Your right-hand side when You come to judge the living and the dead. Amen.*

93. Multiplies five barley loaves and two fishes to feed five thousand. Remnants are gathered into twelve baskets (6:4-13). *Reveals* that His divine mercy and power exceed man's needs and expectations (symbolized by twelve baskets of remnants). The miracle prompted them to say, "This is indeed the prophet who is to come into the world." They sought to proclaim Him

king, but He, disapproving of their motive, left them for His mountain solitude. Shortly after, when they followed Him to Capharnaum, Jesus said to them, "You seek me, not because you have eaten of the loaves and have been filled. Do not labor for the food that perishes, but for that which endures unto life everlasting, which the Son of Man will give you. For upon him, the Father, God himself, has set his seal." Refers to Himself as the bread of heaven for the world and implies His instituting the Holy Eucharist. *Lord, grant us the heavenly bread that gives us eternal life.*

94. Reads Pharisees' minds. Forgives the adulteress they had set up as bait in front of Jesus as they asked Him what He would do with her (8:-11). *Reveals* Pharisees' duplicity. A warning to the adulteress against falling back to sin. "But Jesus, stooping down, began to write with his finger on the ground. But when they continued asking him, he raised himself and said to them, 'Let him who is without sin among you be the first to cast a stone at her.' And again stooping down, he began to write on the ground. But hearing this, they went away one by one . . . And Jesus, said to her, 'Woman, where are they? Has no one condemned thee?' She said, no one, Lord.' Then Jesus said, 'Neither will I condemn thee. Go thy way and from now on, sin no more.'" A remarkably relevant condemnation of self-righteousness and hypocrisy! Shows Christ's infinite mercy on sinners!

95. On a Sabbath, He cures a man born blind. He uses spittle, clay, and the pool waters of Siloe as conduits of His mercy and power. Pharisees intimidate him and his fearful parents (9:1-41). Jesus reveals the man's blindness happened so that *"the works of God* be made manifest." This *reveals* the following:

a) Jesus' works are the works of God the Father who sent Him. Miracles are for the glory of Jesus Christ and His Father.

b) Jesus *reveals* Himself as the light of the world. Just as the blind man needs light to his blindness to be able to see, so does the world need light for it to see His Father. He is the light *sent* (*Siloe* in Hebrew) by the Father. "As long as I am in the world, I am the light of the world," He said. Despite the testimony of his parents and neighbors that it was truly he who was born blind and now could see, the Pharisees repeatedly asked him who it was who had cured him. Unable to tell them, the man said, "You have heard. Why would you hear again? Would you also become his disciples?" They heaped abuse on him and said, "Thou art his disciple, but we are disciples of Moses . . . But as for this man, we do not know where he is from." The man told them, "Why, herein is the marvel, that you do not know where he is from, and yet he opened my eyes. Now we know that God does not hear sinners; but if anyone is a worshipper of God, and does his will, him he hears. Not from the beginning of the world has it been heard that anyone opened the eyes of a man born blind. If this man were not from God, he could do nothing."

c) Jesus *reveals* Himself as the incarnate Son of God. Hearing that they had turned him out, Jesus found him and said to him, "Dost thou believe in the Son of God?" He answered and said, "Who is he, that I may believe in him?" And Jesus said to him, "Thou hast both seen him, and he it is who speaks with thee." And he said, "I believe, Lord." And falling down, he worshipped him. "Lord, we believe."

96. Raises Lazarus from the dead (11:1-44). Lord, raise us from the life of sin and bring us to eternal life! (See essay 1.)

97. Reads thoughts of men, of Judas Iscariot, and of Peter (13:21, 14:30). *Reveals* His omniscience. On Judas' betrayal: "One of you will betray me." On Peter's denial: "I say to thee, the cock will not crow before thou dost deny me thrice." As *Psalm 138 (139)* sings, "O Lord, you have probed me and you know me. You know when I sit and when I stand; you understand my thought from afar. My journeys and my rest you scrutinize, with all my ways you are familiar. Even before a word is on my tongue, behold, O Lord, you know the whole of it. Behind me and before, you hem me in and rest your hand upon me."

Lord, You know my inner thoughts. Deliver me from evil, and make me faithful to You always unto the end. Amen.

98. Soldiers cast lots "to see whose it shall be," for the tunic was without seam, woven in one piece from the top (19:24). *Reveals* Jesus' power on day-to-day living, including concerns about clothing. But this piece was one more sign of the prophetic fulfillment about His passion: "That the Scripture might be fulfilled which says, 'They divided my garments among them; and for my vesture, they cast lots.'" "We believe You are the Redeemer who came down to die for our sins. Cleansed from sin and redeemed with Your blood, we are Yours to bring to the Father in heaven."

99. The resurrection (20:1-18). (See essay 1 and no. 30 above.)

100. On Jesus' urging, the apostles "cast the net *to the right of them[1] and they were unable to draw it up for the great number of fishes . . . And when they had landed, they saw a fire ready, and a fish laid upon it, and bread. Jesus said to them, 'Bring here some of the fishes that you caught just now.' Simon Peter went aboard and hauled the net onto land full of large fishes, one hundred fifty-three in number" (21:5-11). Reveals* Christ's all-knowing power over the sea, the earth, the forces of nature, and the manner by which man can reap their fruits. Lord, give us that living trust in You that we may be with You happily in eternity. Amen.

"And many more signs also Jesus worked in the sight of His disciples which are not written in this book But these are written that you may believe that Jesus is the Christ, the Son of God, and that believing, you may have life in his name" (21:30).

---

[1] It's interesting to read that Jesus pointed to the "*right* of them" as where the apostles would cast the net and draw a "great number of fishes." And is it quite a coincidence that the thief who was promised paradise "today" was on the *right-hand side* of the cross? Also note Matthew 25:34: "Then the King will say to those on his right hand, 'Come, blessed of my Father, take possession of the kingdom prepared for you from the foundation of the world . . .'"

ESSAY 3

Apostolic Miracles

TO CONTINUE TENDING His flock to the end of time, Jesus gathered His apostles and empowered them to preach and perform miracles as He had done from Galilee to Judea. He commanded them to go to all nations, to draw people to Him (Lk 9:44), baptizing them in the name of the Father and of the Son and of the Holy Spirit and teaching them to observe all that He had commanded them (Mt 28:18-20). He assured them that His power would always be with them (Lk 5:17) unto the consummation of the world (Mt 28:18-20). He gave them power to cast out devils in His name, speak in new tongues, and if they drank any deadly thing, it would not hurt them (Mk 16:17-18). He guaranteed that those who believed in them believed in Him also (Lk 10:16) and He would give them eternal life.

But to His apostles whom He was sending out into the world, He gave a warning: the world would hate them, for they were not of this world even as He was not of this world (Jn 16:14). He said, "In the world, you will have affliction" (Jn 16:33). Jesus gave them notice of the fierce opposition His enemies would put up, even causing them their martyrdom. But He said, "Take courage. I have overcome the world" (Jn 16:33). To console and strengthen them, He said the Father would send the advocate in His name who will "convict the world of sin, and of justice, and of judgment." "Of sin, because they do not believe in me; of justice, because I go to the Father, and you will see me no more; and of judgment, because *the prince of this world has already been judged*" (16:10-11).

To fully prepare them to battle Satan, the Holy Spirit would come down to His apostles and teach them all things (Jn 14:26) and bring to their minds whatever He had said to them. Thus, armed with the wisdom of the Spirit and the power of the Father and the Son, the apostles would go forth fearlessly into the world, preaching, casting out devils, and performing miracles.

We can't imagine how many miracles the twelve apostles performed. Neither could anyone estimate how many books would have been written to record them, considering the fact that the apostles spread out to "all nations"—from what is known today as the Middle East, including Northern Africa, to as far as Spain (possibly, Britain in the West) and India in the East—preaching, casting out devils, and making miracles as Jesus had commissioned them to do. There were some written reports of early apostolic miracles, including those classified as apocryphal, but only *The Acts of the Apostles*, written by St. Luke the Evangelist, is included among the inspired books of the Bible. A companion of St. Paul in the apostle's journey from Palestine to Rome, St. Luke (a physician by profession and acknowledged as an artist) was an eyewitness to a lot of the miracles he recorded in the *Acts*. Obviously, the *Acts* is not a book about all the miracles done by the apostles, but it presents an important account of the beginnings of the church and the apostles' missionary effort among the gentiles, particularly those of Sts. Peter and Paul. But as always, these miracles, wherever they were performed, were done to show God's infinite power and mercy and to convey messages related to man's salvation.

The Twelve Apostles (Mt 10:3-4)

St. Peter—Born in Bethsaida, Galilee, he grew up as a fisherman but lived in Capharnaum. His mother-in-law lived, who lived with him and his wife was cured by Jesus. On Peter (from the Greek word for *rock*), Jesus founded His church. Peter witnessed all His miracles, including the transfiguration, the raising of Jairus' daughter back to life, and the miraculous catch. Jesus paid the temple tax for him. Peter witnessed His agony in Gethsemane and His arrest and the cure of the high priest's servant's ear. He exemplified regret for denying his master and saw Him risen. Christ endowed him with the power to tend His sheep (primacy). He presided over the selection of Matthias to replace Judas Iscariot. After the descent of the Holy Spirit, he delivered his first sermon that stirred up thousands to convert and be baptized. He cured the paralytic at the steps of the temple and brought life back to Tabitha, a faithful, charitable Christian woman. He converted the centurion Cornelius and defended his decision to bring the gentiles into the church. He did missionary work in Asia Minor and was martyred by Nero in Rome between AD 64 and 67. On his burial spot in Rome now stands St. Peter's Basilica (*ES*).

St. Andrew—Brother of St. Peter, he was born in Bethsaida but lived in Capharnaum. He was a fisherman and former disciple of St. John the Baptist. He was the one who brought the boy with the five loaves to Jesus (Jn 6:8). He preached in Southern Russia and was martyred in Greece (*ES*).

St. James (called the Greater because he was taller in stature than the other St. James)—Son of Zebedee and Salome. Fisherman, whose fiery personality and apostolic zeal earned him, with his brother John, the title "Son of Thunder." Preached in Jerusalem where he was killed by order of King Agrippa, a fierce defender of the Jewish faith, between AD 42 and 44 (*ES*).

St. John—Born in Bethsaida in the year 6, son of Zebedee and Salome and brother of James. Was a former disciple of St. John the Baptist. Was present at the multiplication of bread and other miracles of Jesus. Witnessed the transfiguration. Seated next to Jesus at the Last Supper. Remained close to Him and stood by the cross. Jesus entrusted His mother to him. With Peter, he was first to go to the tomb; he was also first to recognize Jesus standing on the shore. Present at the descent of the Holy Spirit. Went to Samaria with St. Peter, imprisoned there, and escaped with the angel's intervention.

NICHOLAS LLANES ROSAL, STD, PHL, MSJ

Preached in Parthia and Ephesus. Attended the council in years 49 (or 50) and 62. Arrested in year 95, brought to Rome, and thrown into a burning cauldron of oil but escaped unscathed. Poisoned by high priest Diana (poison arising from the chalice in the form of a serpent) but was unharmed according to St. Mark's words (16:18). Exiled to Patmos where he wrote the *Revelation*, was released, and went to Ephesus where he died in AD 100. He wrote the fourth gospel and three epistles (*ES*).

St. Philip—Born in Bethsaida. Was a former disciple of St. John the Baptist. Brought Bartholomew to Jesus. Preached in Greece. Crucified head down in Phrygia in the year AD 80. He cast out the devil from an idol that crumbled. According to tradition, he slew a dragon (*ES*).

St. Bartholomew—Known as Nathaniel, a native of Cana. Was introduced by Philip to Jesus. Preached in Mesopotamia, Egypt, and the shores of the Black Sea. Was martyred by Albanopolis in Armenia for converting King Polymius (brother of the murderer). Flayed alive then beheaded. Other accounts say he was crucified head down. Patron of tanners (*ES*).

St. Thomas—Born in Galilee. Known as Doubting Thomas (Jn 20:27). When the lot fell to him to go to India, he complained that he was "too ill to go" and that not even Jesus' apparition would make him go. Christ appeared to a merchant, Abbon by name, who sold Thomas into slavery to become a carpenter for the Indian king Gundafor. On his way to India, he built churches and parishes. The king gave him twenty pieces of silver to finance a castle, but Thomas, instead, gave the money to the poor. He was imprisoned and sentenced to be flayed alive. Meanwhile, according to the apocryphal *Acts of Thomas*, the king's brother died, and seeing the place in heaven intended for his royal brother on account of Thomas' good deeds, the brother asked permission to come back to earth to purchase his brother's spot for himself. The king not only refused but also released Thomas and converted to Christianity.

However true this story might be, Christians in Kerala claim they were converted by Thomas. According to some accounts, the Saint was martyred in AD 72 after converting many in the city of King Misdai. Four soldiers were said to have pierced him with their spears. Christians buried him in the tomb of ancient kings (*ES*).

In the Gospel of St. John, St. Thomas is reported as doubting the resurrection of Christ, saying, "Except I see in his hands the print of the nails, and put my finger into the print of the nails, and thrust my hand into his side, I will not believe." Eight days later, Jesus appeared to him and said, "Reach hinder thy finger and behold my hands, and reach hither thy hand and thrust it into my side, and be not faithless, but believing." And the Saint, prostrating, exclaimed, "My Lord and My God."

St. Matthew—The publican and tax collector in Capharnaum. Invited Jesus to dinner in his home where Pharisees thought to themselves how Jesus, if He was the all-knowing Messiah, could let Himself associate with a taxpayer whose job was hated by all. Preached in Persia and Macedonia. Martyred in year 120. Wrote the first gospel (*ES*).

St. James the Less—Son of Alpheus and Mary, a close relative of the Virgin Mary, and brother of St. Jude. Probably a first cousin of Jesus. Jews called him James the Just. Abstained from meat and wine. Attended the Council of Jerusalem in the year 49 or 50 where he defended St. Peter's teaching that Christian Jews were exempt from circumcision. Died in AD 62 in Jerusalem. Thrown from the temple pinnacle by the Pharisees. Catastrophes that visited Jerusalem after his death were attributed by the people as divine punishment for his death. Wrote an epistle exhorting Jewish Christians to persevere. First bishop of Jerusalem. Called Patron of the Dying for forgiving his murderers at his deathbed (*ES*).

St. Jude—Son of Alpheus and Mary, brother of St. James the Less, and first cousin of Jesus. A fisherman. Wrote an epistle about perseverance and purity of the faith. Evangelized Persia. Expelled demons from idols, leaving them crumbling. With St. Simon, he was beheaded with a short sickle-shaped sword. Patron of desperate situations, hopeless and impossible causes, and hospitals (*ES*).

St. Simeon (the *Canaanaean*)—Born in Galilee. Was called the Zealot for his zeal for Jewish law. Evangelized the Black Sea area, North Africa, and Britain. Probably worked with St. Jude in Persia. Also said to have succeeded St. James as bishop of Jerusalem. Legend says he was sawed in half by pagan priests (*ES*).

St. Matthias—Became an apostle to replace Judas Iscariot. Was chosen by lot (Acts 1:15-26) by the apostles with St. Peter presiding. Joseph, who was called Barsabbas, was the other candidate, but through the inspiration of the Holy Spirit, St. Matthias was chosen. Nothing more is known about this new apostle although it's presumed that he went out to evangelize many communities as instructed by St. Peter (*ES*).

Miracles in the Acts of the Apostles

1. The Pentecost. Coming down in the form of parted tongues of fire, the Holy Spirit (1:5) baptized the apostles and made them speak in foreign languages (2:4).

    a. *Reveals* the Holy Spirit as a distinct third person of the Holy Trinity. Through the apostles, the Holy Spirit prompted three thousand people to repent and to be baptized on the first day and five thousand the following day.
    b. *Manifests* the essential role of the Holy Spirit in the church as guide and guardian of the "body of Christ" (1 Cor 12:27). He animates everyone "member for member"—beginning with the apostles then following with the prophets, the teachers, and the "ministers of miracles" and other services.
    c. *Shows* (1) the Holy Spirit as *the sanctifying power* that purifies men of sin through baptism, thereby effecting the salvation

of individual believers, in particular, and the world, in general; (2) the Holy Spirit as the *power behind the miracles* of the apostles, future disciples, and saints until the end of time; and (3) the Holy Spirit *who, by fire, would be anointed unto all the disciples to come* (Mt 3:16; Mk 1:10; Lk 3:22; Jn 1:32).

2. Apostles speak in foreign tongues. Jews from "every nation under heaven" were bewildered to hear each speaking in his own language (Acts 2:5-6). *Reveals* the Holy Spirit as source of the twin power of speaking and understanding. As the divine communicator, He gives man not only the courage *to think and speak* the right things but also *the ability to hear and receive* the right message. The Spirit brings peace among people, linking speaker and hearer.

3. Apostles Peter and John cure a forty-year-old beggar, who, lame from his mother's womb, lay at the temple gate begging. When the two apostles saw him, Peter said, "Look at us." He looked at them, hoping to receive something from them, but Peter said, "Silver and gold I have none, but what I have, that I give thee. In the name of Jesus Christ of Nazareth, arise and walk." And taking him by the right hand, Peter raised him up, and immediately his feet and ankles became strong. "Leaping up and praising God, he went with them into the temple" (3:1-10). *Reveals* the apostles' miraculous ability to cure and shows the power of the name of the risen Jesus. After angry authorities arrested and kept them in custody because they had spoken in the temple about resurrection and the name of Jesus, Peter and John appeared before the high priest Annas, the elders, and the Sadducees (who did not believe in resurrection). To them, Peter said, "If we are on trial today about a good work done to a cripple as to how this man has been cured, be it known . . . that in the name of Jesus Christ of Nazareth whom you crucified, whom God has raised from the dead, even in this name does He stand here before you, sound. This is 'the stone that was rejected by you, the builders, which has become the

NICHOLAS LLANES ROSAL, STD, PHL, MSJ

cornerstone.' Neither is there salvation in any other. *For **there is no other name** under heaven given to men by whom we must be saved.*"

(Reflection: We note how Annas, the elders, and the officials reacted to Peter's discourse: "Now, seeing the boldness of Peter and John, and *finding that they were uneducated and ordinary men,* they began to marvel and to recognize them as having been with Jesus. And seeing the man who had been cured standing with them, they could say nothing in reply" [4:13-14]. Here was the Holy Spirit at work, making simple, uneducated men trump the elite, the mighty, and the wise men of Jerusalem. Manifested herein was the divine presence of Jesus in and with His apostles. *See here how a lame man's mere presence leaped to stun Christ's enemies into silence!* Unable to answer Peter and powerless to deny the miracle, the Sanhedrin decided just to warn Peter and John to speak no more about Jesus' name. To this, Peter and John said, "Whether it is right in the sight of God to listen to you rather than to God, decide for yourselves. For we cannot but speak of what we have seen and heard.")

4. Peter reads the minds of Ananias and his wife, who, lying, keep part of the money (from the sale of their land) they had pledged for the primitive church-community's support. (Many believers then lived together to form communes, supported by members' assets.) Peter condemns the lie, and the couple dies at his feet (5:1-31). *Reveals* that nothing is hidden from the Holy Spirit ("Quidquid latet aparebit" or "Whatever is hidden will be made open.") Be honest. Shows the apostles' authority.

5. "Now, **by the hands of the apostles, many signs and wonders were done** among the people . . . And the multitude of men and women who believed in the Lord increased still more so that they carried the sick into the streets and laid them on beds and pallets that, *when Peter passed, his shadow at least might fall on some of them.* And there came also multitudes from the towns near Jerusalem, bringing the sick and those troubled with unclean spirits, and they were all cured" (Acts 5:12-16).

Reveals the continuing presence of Christ in the world—as He had promised—through his apostles' miracles.

6. Filled with jealousy over the apostles' miracles, the high priest and the party of the Sadducees "seized the apostles and put them in the public prison. But during the night, **an angel of the Lord opened the doors of the prison and led them out,** saying, 'Go, stand and speak in the temple to the people all the words of this life.' And when they heard this, they went into the temple about daybreak and began to teach" (5:17-21). *Reveals* that angels provide special protection over ministers of God.

7. "Then, all who sat in the Sanhedrin gazing upon him (Stephen, the deacon) saw **his face as though it were the face of an angel**" (6:15). We read in St. Paul's letter to the Hebrews (1:6) how God can make angels appear as winds or flames of fire. *Reveals* it behooved that an angel change the face of Stephen— who was "full of the Spirit" and "full of grace and power" (6:8, 7:34)—to enhance his authority before the Sanhedrin. Recalling the prophecies from Abraham to Solomon, Stephen said, "Stiff-necked in heart and ear, you always oppose the Holy Spirit, as your fathers did . . . . Which of the prophets have not your fathers persecuted? And they killed those who foretold the coming of the Just One, of whom you have now been the betrayers and murderers, you who received the law as an ordinance of angels and did not keep it" (7:51-53). Shows the important role of the deacons in the early church and today's as well.

8. Visiting Lydda, Peter cures Aeneas, a paralytic for eight years. "Peter said to him, 'Aeneas, Jesus Christ heals thee. Get up and make thy bed.' And straightway, he got up" (9:33). *Reveals* that God cures whom He *wills* to cure. Miracle leads to mass conversion. "And all who lived at Lydda and in Sharon saw him and they turned to the Lord."

9. Peter brings Tabitha (devoted her life to good works and acts of love) back to life. "All the widows stood around him weeping and showing him the tunics and cloaks Tabitha made for them . . . Putting them all out, he (Peter) knelt down and

prayed and turning to the body, said, 'Tabitha. Arise.' And she opened her eyes and, seeing Peter, she sat up." *Reveals* that many, touched by miracles, believed in the Lord (9:37-42). Tabitha's good works were a welcome preparation for a miracle.

10. Saul makes Elymas, a sorcerer, blind for "trying to turn the pro-consul away from the faith." Sergius Paulus, the proconsul, had sent for Saul (Paul) and Barnabas to hear the word of God, but Elymas tried to keep them away. "Saul, filled with the Holy Spirit, gazed at him and said, 'O full of all guile and of all deceit, son of the devil, enemy of all justice, wilt thou not cease to make crooked the straight ways of the Lord? . . . Behold, the hand of the Lord is upon thee, and thou shalt be blind not seeing the sun for a time.' And instantly there fell upon him a mist of darkness and he groped about for someone to lead him by the hand." *Reveals* "the proconsul, seeing what had happened, believed and was astonished at the Lord's teaching" (13:8-11). People who block the work of God will be meted out just punishment. Miracle leads to conversion.

11. In Lystra, a man, crippled from birth, listened to Paul. Gazing at him and *seeing that he had faith to be cured*, Paul said with a loud voice, "Stand upright on thy feet." And he sprang up and began to walk. Then the crowds, seeing what Paul had done, lifted up their voice, saying, "The gods have come down to us in the likeness of men." They called Barnabas as Jupiter and Paul as Mercury. And the priest of Jupiter brought garlands and oxen and would have offered a sacrifice had not Paul stopped them, saying, "We also are mortals, human beings like you." And he went on to explain the faith about Jesus Christ, exhorting them to "turn away from vain things to the living God." But then, the Jews arrived from Antioch and Iconium and won the crowds over to their side. They dragged and stoned Paul and left him for dead until he stood up and reentered the city (14:18). *Reveals* God's special protection over Paul and the disciples. Manifests widespread paganism—a fertile ground for preaching and conversion. Yet as the harvest was about to start, the jealous Jews came to block it. Shows

devils are always around to oppose the spread of the kingdom of God.

12. Paul casts out devil from a slave girl, a soothsayer used by her masters for profit. The devil and the money-making soothsaying business gone, the slave girl's masters went to the magistrates, who ordered Paul and Silas to be beaten with rods then thrown into the inner jail with feet fastened in the stocks. *"But at midnight, Paul and Silas were praying, singing the praises of the Lord, and the prisoners were listening to them, and suddenly, there was such a great earthquake that the foundations of the prison flew open, and everyone's chains were unfastened. And the jailer, roused from out of sleep and seeing that the doors of the prison were open, drew his sword and was about to kill himself, thinking that the prisoners had escaped. But Paul cried with a loud voice, saying, 'Do thyself no harm, for we are all here.' Then calling for light, he ran in and trembling for fear fell down before Paul and Silas, and bringing them out, he said, 'Sirs, what must I do to be saved?' And they said, 'Believe in the Lord Jesus, and thou shalt be saved, and thy household.' And they spoke the word of the Lord to him and to all who were in the household. And he took them at that very hour of the night and washed their wounds immediately. And taking them into his house, he set food before them, and rejoiced with all his household over his faith in God"* (16:25-34). Miracles *reveal* divine justice. They lead to conversions and manifest the power of prayer, especially one that sings the praises of the Lord.

13. In Ephesus, Paul baptizes twelve men (who had been baptized by John with the baptism of repentance), and they began to speak in tongues and to prophesy (19:5-7). *Reveals* that repentance from sin prepares people to receive the Holy Spirit.

14. "And **God worked more than the usual miracles by the hand of Paul, so that even handkerchiefs and aprons were carried from his body to the sick, and the diseases left them and the evil spirits went out**" (19:11-12). *Reveals* that items connected with the holy man become conduits of miraculous power. Basis for the veneration of relics.

15. *"Certain of the itinerant Jewish exorcists also attempted to invoke the name of the Lord Jesus over those who had evil spirits in them, saying, 'I adjure you by the Jesus whom Paul preaches.' And a certain Sceva, a Jewish high priest, had seven sons who were doing this. But the evil spirit answered and said to them, 'Jesus I acknowledge and Paul I know, but who are you?' And the man in whom the evil spirit was, sprang at them and overpowered them both with such violence that they fled from that home tattered and bruised. And* **this became known** *to all the Jews and Gentiles living in Ephesus and fear fell on them all, and* **the name of the Lord Jesus came to be held in high honor**" (19:13-18).

16. Paul brings life back to Eutychus, a young man who fell from a third-floor window as he was overcome with drowsiness while listening to Paul's address that started from the *breaking of bread* to midnight (20:8-12). "And they took away the boy alive and were not a little comforted."

17. An angel appears to Paul, assuring him of his safety and of the 276 passengers aboard the ship in the midst of a raging storm on his way to Rome. *"Arriving safe on the island of Malta but cold from the storm at sea, Paul gathered a bundle of sticks and laid them on the fire when a viper came out because of the heat and fastened on his hand. When the natives saw the creature hanging from his hand, they said to one another, 'Surely, this man is a murderer, for though he has escaped the sea, Justice does not let him live.' But he shook off the creature into the fire and suffered no harm. They were expecting that he would swell up and suddenly fall down and die; but after waiting a long time seeing no harm come to him, they changed their minds and said that he was a god"* (28:2-7). *Reveals* God's design for Paul to reach Rome—world center of the gentiles—where God wanted him to spread the word of salvation.

18. Paul cures the father of Publius, the island's headman, of fever and dysentery. *"After this, all the sick on the island came and were cured"* (28:8-10). *Reveals* the apostle used his miraculous power to express gratitude for the people's kindness and for God's mercy.

St. Paul reached Rome, the great gentile city. Kept there in chains for two years, "he welcomed all who came to him, preaching the Kingdom of God and teaching about the Lord Jesus Christ with all boldness and unhindered" (Acts 28:30-31). According to tradition, he was finally released, then he traveled to Spain (Rom 15:24, 15:28) but went back to Rome where he was imprisoned again. Finally, like St. Peter and the rest of the apostles, St. Paul received the crown of martyrdom. Now in heaven, Sts. Peter and Paul and the other apostles keep the miraculous power that Christ had given them so that they can continue helping people on earth *with their miracles*. Holy apostles, pray for us. Amen.

NICHOLAS LLANES ROSAL, STD, PHL, MSJ

ACKNOWLEDGMENT

T HE WRITER GRATEFULLY acknowledges the sources listed below for the information on miracles included in the following essay 4, "Miracles and the Saints":

Heavenly Friends by Rosalie Marie Levy. St. Paul Editions, Boston, Massachusetts, 1979. (Miracles from this source will be cited as *HF.*)

The Encyclopedia of Saints by Rosemary Ellen Gulley. Checkmark Books, New York, New York, 2001.[2] (Miracles from this source will be cited as *ES.*)

The Saint and Mother of all Times

Our Lady of Lourdes

---

[2] Thanks to Mr. Gilbert Streeter, a good neighbor, for lending this helpful book to the writer and for troubleshooting the writer's computer glitches.

ESSAY 4

Miracles and the Saints

THROUGH HIS DISCIPLES over the centuries, Christ has continued preaching His kingdom and performing miracles in the world as He did in Galilee two thousand years ago. Today, His message is being preached and His miracles are being performed in the six continents of the world, where over one billion people have been baptized in His name. His compassionate love has not changed because it is infinite and eternal. He made humans His instruments to spread His message and perform miracles because His humanity was the medium of His divinity to pour His love on all in the world. From among mankind, He chose a few to be His apostles and charged them to bring others into His church—His body. Into this body, His apostles brought men and women to become the light of the world, to mirror Christ's life of love, *to explain His teachings by their lives,* and to use the gifts of the Holy Spirit received in baptism and confirmation. He loves them. They love Him in return, thereby making their lives a reflection of Christ's life—the life that dispensed love and goodness to the world. These are men and women we call Saints. To them, Christ grants the Holy Spirit's special gifts of tongues and miracles, for as St. Paul writes, "We know that in everything, God works for good with those who love him" (Rom 8:28). Above all, *miracles are Christ's gifts of love to mankind.*

The stories we read below represent a tiny fraction of the number of recorded and unrecorded miracles of Saints over the centuries. But they tell us how the Saints followed Christ's overpowering message revealed by the miracles: *Follow him to Calvary* like Mary His mother, John the Beloved, and Mary Magdalene. "That is the message of Christ's miracles," the loved Jesuit preacher Father Freddy Balinong said, impressing that message upon his cosmopolitan New York congregation. Indeed, didn't Jesus say, "If any man will come after me, let him deny himself, and take up his cross daily, and follow me" (Lk 9:23)? This is the *way of life,* the way to Calvary, He laid out for them—for us all—to reach resurrection day!

Those who follow Jesus to Calvary find the strength to suffer despite the human inclination to avoid suffering. Yet we'll see in the lives of the Saints that they did not only gladly suffer for Christ, but they also tried to find ways to suffer more for His sake. We see this at the end of St. Lawrence's life, who, already dying on a burning iron bed, still asked his executioners to turn him to the other side of his body so that his body could burn entirely and suffer more. We also see this unbelievable courage in the children of Fátima, who vied with one another to invent ways to suffer more for Jesus. St. Francis of Assisi renounced the life of luxury he was to enjoy from his inheritance and embraced poverty instead to be able to suffer for Christ. From their sufferings, the Saints became living likenesses of the crucified Jesus. Crucified, Jesus used the power of the cross to perform miracles, converting the thief on his right side and causing the elements to express sorrow over His sufferings. Following Christ to Calvary, the Saints embraced the cross, received its power, and used it to perform miracles to help others find their way to heavenly paradise.

With the power the Saints received for following Christ to Calvary, they performed miracles to help bring salvation to countless people. They brought the spiritually dead souls back to the life of grace and even raised the physically dead back to life because behind every miracle they performed was a salvation-related message. They read minds and prophesied to prepare others to accept God's will. To show God's compassion and give them strength to do His will, they multiplied food and cured people of their illnesses. They walked on water, conquered fire, and influenced the elements to confirm their preaching about God's power. With their miracles, they defied the enemies of God to prove the trustworthiness of the truth they preached. Their power to levitate and shine showed their intimate union with Christ. They spoke in tongues to testify to the authority of the Holy Spirit over every word of their preaching. Their relics became conduits of the power Jesus granted them to show they were one with Him. Jesus appeared and talked to them. So did Mary, His mother, to show the Saints were one family with them. All these came to pass so that, in the name of Jesus, others will be saved and glorify God here and in eternity.

They Brought the Dead Back to Life

As a regiment entered the gate of Amiens in Northern France, a beggar, "shivering in the deadly cold winter of 355, extended his hand for alms. No one stopped except a young officer who dismounted from his horse, drew his sword to cut his cloak in half and gave the other half to the beggar. 'It's all I have to give,' he said, 'I have no money.' That night, the officer saw Christ in a dream. Wearing the other half on His shoulders, He told the officer, 'Look at this cloak, and see if you recognize it.' Then, turning from the officer to a host of Angels, Christ said, 'Though only a catechumen, Martin has clothed me with this garment.'"

Martin of Tours soon asked to be baptized. A few years later, he was given by St. Hilary, the local bishop, a piece of land where Martin built a monastery. People went there, seeking to be baptized. Returning briefly to Hungary, his native land, he converted his mother to Christianity. Upon his arrival in his monastery, he found the young man whom he had been preparing for baptism dead. Asking to be alone with the dead body, Martin prayed earnestly and lay himself on the dead young man as Elijah (1 Kgs 17:20-24) and Elias (3 Kgs 17:21) had done to raise the dead back to life. The dead youth came back to life, was baptized, and lived a long life. St.

Martin died in 397. His relics, preserved in several European cities, became objects of pilgrimages (*HF*).

The Saint's miracle is among the countless life-giving miracles in the history of the church. Recorded among them was the miracle by *St. Ambrose,* bishop of Milan. Like St. Martin and the Old Testament prophets, he spread himself over the body of Decentius, son of Florence, and the dead young man came back to life. When St. Ambrose discovered the tombs of Gervase and Protase, people who touched their relics were healed. Severus, a blind butcher, touched the relics with his handkerchief, applied it to his eyes, and immediately began to see (*ES*).

With holy water and prayer, *St. Dominic,* founder of the Dominican Order, raised three dead persons from the dead, including a cardinal's nephew who had been thrown off a horse and died (*HF/ES*).

St. Francis of Assisi brought back to life a woman who appeared before God and was about to be sentenced when the Saint intervened. The woman came back to earth, did penance, was given a priest's absolution, and then passed on to the next life. In Voltiano, a young man drowned. His family asked him to intercede, and hardly had they finished their prayers when the young man came back to life. While still alive, St. Francis cured a paralytic by the sign of the cross and healed a crippled young man, the son of a gentleman in whose house he briefly stayed. St. Francis performed many other miracles (*ES*).

One day, the king slandered *St. Stanislaus,* bishop of Poland, claiming that the Saint had not paid for the land he had purchased. St. Stanislaus brought the seller back from the grave to appear in court. (The Saint subsequently excommunicated the king for the slander.) *St. Louis Bertrand*—a native of Valencia, Spain; blood relative of St. Vincent Ferrer; and Dominican missionary to South America, where he baptized thousands (fifteen thousand alone in Monpaia)—raised a dead woman to life. *St. Remigius*—archbishop of Rheims who baptized Clovis, king of the Franks—raised a dead girl to life (*HF*).

St. Nicholas of Bari was archbishop of Myra when famine struck the country. Visiting different towns and villages in his diocese, St. Nicholas multiplied bread and distributed them to the hungry families. On one of those journeys, he lodged at the home of a man who fed tourists. When he sat down to eat, St. Nicholas observed that the meat in his plate had an unusually different texture, causing him to inquire about this unusual kind of meat. Confused and trembling, the host admitted that due to the exhausted source of regular food supply, he stole and murdered children, prepared them, and then served their flesh as meat to travelers. The Saint then walked to the place where salted remains of young victims were kept. Making the sign of the cross over them, three little children came back to life. The Saint died a martyr for the faith. Many years later, his body was moved to Bari, Italy. He became patron Saint of children and is celebrated today as Santa Claus (*HF*).

Miracles proved the Saints' kinship with Christ, who shared His power to convert sinners. In them, "the power of the Lord was present" (Lk 5:17). By the power of their holy lives, they preached the teachings of the Lord: about *love of neighbor,* seen in St. Martin's act of kindness; about *proclaiming the truth,* exemplified by St. Ambrose's and St. Dominic's work against heretics; about *honesty and truthfulness,* shown in St. Stanislaus' action against the king; about *baptism,* shown in St. Louis' missionary work in South America and St. Remigius' preaching among the Franks and Goths; and about *justice and compassion*, especially for children, exemplified by St. Nicholas. The Saints bore good fruits, according to St. Luke: "For there is no good tree that bears bad fruit, nor is there a bad tree that bears good fruit" (6:43-45).

They Read Minds and Prophesied

Jesus' power to read minds and prophesy was also given to the Saints. *St. Joseph Cupertino,* known for his miraculous ability to fly (amazed the Spanish ambassador and his attendants in church by flying over them to a statue of Mary), could smell unconfessed sins

(*ES*). *St. Mariana of Quito* prophesied the hour and day of her death. *Padre Pio* had knowledge of secrets of people who hid them (*ES*).

St. Rose of Viterbo prophesied the exact day of the unexpected death of the emperor. The Saints' prophetic miracles reveal the powerful presence of the Holy Spirit, who speaks through the Saints to guide and prepare people to meet the future, especially the hour of death. Prophetic vision stresses Jesus' warning: "Watch, therefore, for you do not know at what hour your Lord is to come" (Mt 24:42). *St. Gerard Majella,* a disciple of St. Alphonsus Ligouri, knew when people didn't confess all that they were supposed to confess. Whoever they were, he would send them back to the confessional. *St. Gemma Galgani* would become physically ill whenever a sinful person was near her (*HF*).

They Multiplied Food, Even Helped With Money

Like Jesus who multiplied bread and fish in the desert, the Saints, given Christ's compassionate power, provided food and other kinds of help for the needy. In need of food for the orphanage he had founded, *St. John Vianney* took a relic of *St. Francis Regis,* placed it by a small pile of corn, and prayed with the children. Shortly after, he found the attic full of corn. *St. Therese of Lisieux* appeared to her prioress in a dream: the two went to an Italian Carmelite convent that was in terrible need of money. In the dream, they placed five hundred francs inside a box. The following morning, the Italian nuns, thousands of miles away, found the money on a parlor table (*ES*).

The St. Sixtus friary's dining room was ready to feed the brothers, but there was no food to serve. *St. Dominic* prayed, and suddenly, two handsome young men appeared carrying loads of bread. They gave each brother a loaf then disappeared (*ES*).

There was no money to buy bread for the convent nuns in Lima. *St. Rose,* trusting that God would never abandon them, opened the chest. There, she found what she had hoped to see.

They had run out of money to buy honey. St. Rose, trusting in God's providence, went to the pantry. Behold, she found eight months' supply of honey! Unwavering faith, with prayer and hope, is key to God's provident love (*ES*).

St. Zita was only twelve years old when she started working as a housekeeper for a rich family in Lucca. Her coworkers disliked her because she worked very hard and went to church every morning. She even helped the poor with foodstuff from her master's food-supply room. She became worried one day when her master was going to check his stock of beans he intended to sell. Behold! The supply was replenished. Working forty-eight years for the Fatinelli family, she never failed to visit the sick and prisoners and attend mass every day. One day, she overstayed in church and was now late to bake bread. When she returned home, "she found loaves of bread neatly laid out in rows in the kitchen." Coworkers, whose hearts she eventually won, sometimes saw an angel doing the baking and cleaning for her (*ES*). Didn't the Lord say, "Seek first the kingdom of God and his justice, and all these things shall be given you besides" (Mt 6:33)?

Their Faith Let Water Burst Forth from Dry Land: A Forest Turned into a Garden

Water, source of life, is one of the most precious gifts God has provided the world. Lack of it, as in deserts and parched land, has caused death to many. Hence, the miraculous power that makes water burst forth from dry land is a special gift of providence that testifies to God's love for mankind. On the island of Lough Carra, Ireland, *St. Fursey* found that his monastery needed clean water. Praying to God, he struck the ground with his staff, and a fountain of clean water burst forth that served his monastery and the entire town (*ES*).

St. Isidore of Madrid maintained a steadfast faith in God despite the jealous farmers who, seeing that he could plow twice as much as they within the same period of time, accused him of getting an extra help they didn't have. They didn't know that an angel was his helper. But the fruits of his labor he divided into three: one for the poor, another for the church, and the rest for himself and his wife, Maria de la Cabeza (who became a saint). In need of water to irrigate his master's land, he struck the ground with his staff, and water came gushing forth. The water, having healing powers, became an object of pilgrimages (*ES*).

St. Cuthbert of Southern Scotland was a Benedictine priest who spent his time tending the sick, instructing poor people, and helping sinners mend their ways. Becoming bishop of Lindisfarne, he banished the devils from the island of Inner Farne and caused a spring to appear out of the stony ground. He changed the taste of water into wine and healed people with holy water (*ES*).

When the blind old priest could not find water to baptize the infant Patrick, the priest took the infant's hand and, with it, made a sign of the cross on the ground, and immediately, water gushed forth. The priest's eyes opened, and he baptized the infant *Patrick, the future apostle of Ireland* (*ES*).

St. Narcissus, who was consecrated bishop of Jerusalem at the age of eighty, had no oil for the lamps of the church for the celebration of Holy Saturday. Asking water to be brought to him, the bishop said a prayer over it, and the water became oil (*ES*).

St. Faro, bishop of Faro in France, gave *St. Fiacre* a forest to clear and own. Instead of using a plow to clean the ground and cutting the trees with an ax, St. Fiacre waved his staff, and the forest became an open field. There, he built a hostel for Irish pilgrims. As water was made available through the miraculous staff, St. Fiacre built a garden where he grew vegetables to feed the poor. The miracles show how God can draw life-giving water out of hard, stony land and can turn a forest into a garden and land for a pilgrims' inn. They paint a picture of how a soul hardened by sin can turn into a living image of Christ through repentance and penance (*ES*).

Water Obeyed Them

To avoid an occasion of sin, *St. Raymond of Peñafort* asked the king to let him leave the island to where the Saint had been asked to accompany him. When the king refused and imposed severe punishment on anyone who helped the priest leave, the Saint walked to the shore. He spread his cloak on the waters and tied one end to his staff for a sail, then after making the sign of the cross, he stepped on the piece of clothing, and off he went riding the sea. In six hours, he reached the shores of Barcelona (*HF*).

St. John of Matha founded the Holy Trinity Religious Order to ransom slaves. Having 120 of them aboard a ship, he was ready to set sail from Tunis when the angry slave owners came on the vessel, removed the helm, and tore the sails. The Saint knelt with a crucifix in his hand and prayed then told his companions to hang their cloaks for sails. The winds took them into Ostia, Rome (*HF*).

Every morning, *St. Germaine,* a poor shepherd girl in Toulouse, France, walked for miles to attend mass. Before going to church, she would plant her staff in front of the sheepfold in a meadow haunted by wolves, and the sheep would stand still in triangle formation until she came back from church. To reach the church, she had to cross a stream that, on some days, "became a raging torrent." On those days, as she approached the stream, the waters would part—to the amazement of neighbors—and she would walk through without getting wet. Seeing the marvel and her other miracles (she was seen to levitate and shine in her small room in a barn), many neighbors who had disliked her because of her physical deformity repented and became more kind (*HF*).

Inspired by the ascetic life of the Egyptian hermit St. Anthony, *St. Hilarion* sold all his possessions, donned a hair shirt, and went into solitude. In the Gaza desert, he performed miracles, curing the sick and causing rain to come down when asked. As the Saint journeyed by visiting places where St. Anthony had stayed, the emperor ordered his arrest. He was in Italy when the earthquake in 366 struck. The people, afraid of a tsunami, pleaded with him for help. Kneeling in the sand, he made three crosses, and the waves calmed down (*ES*).

St. Hyacinth, born in Poland, received the religious habit from St. Dominic himself. Ordained as a priest, he preached in Northern Europe, Russia, China, and Tibet. While traveling with three companions, he came to the Vistula River. On the other side was a large group of people waiting for them. No boat to carry him and his companions over, he made the sign of the cross and, with his companions, walked on the water to meet the people (*ES*).

As a five-year-old, *St. John of the Cross,* while playing, fell into a lake and sank to the bottom. He saw a beautiful lady who offered him a hand to help, but he refused to take it because his fingers were muddy. He climbed to the surface with the help of a farmer's pole. The Saint attributed the rescue to the Blessed Virgin (*ES*).

St. Francis of Paola, founder of the Minim Friars, was offered gold coins by King Ferrantes of Naples to help build a monastery. Taking a coin and breaking it in two, blood dropped out of the halves. The Saint told him the blood was blood squeezed out of his subjects. The corrupt king became penitent. His miracles confirmed his teaching on honesty. He struck the ground with his staff, and sweet healing water gushed forth. He multiplied food and wine, controlled the elements, read minds, prophesied, and made himself invisible when traveling (*HF*).

Walking one day on the Neapolitan shore, *St. Gerard Majella* saw a ship about to capsize during a sudden squall. People cried as he made the sign of the cross and told the boat captain to stop. He took off his cloak, laid it on the water, walked to the boat, and pulled it to safety. A mystic, the Saint often fell into ecstasy, levitated, and glowed—becoming almost like the sun. He was frequently bruised by devils but cured himself with holy water. He was more than once seen flying over a quarter of a mile (*ES*).

St. Rita of Cascia was married to an abusive man who made her life miserable. When the marriage ended with his death eighteen years later, she tried to pursue her desire to be a nun—a vocation she felt when she was only twelve—but the Augustinian convent she was eager to enter refused to accept her. She did not fit the requirement: she had to be a virgin. After repeated and persistent requests to be admitted, she was finally accepted. To test her obedience, the superior gave her a dry stick to plant and *water every day*—to the amusement of the nuns. A year passed, and the stick grew tall, blooming and growing grapes. Its leaves were ground and given to the sick; cures took place. Her devotion to the passion of Christ was so intense that she asked Him for a thorn to be transplanted from His crown to her forehead. Christ gave it to her, and the thorn caused a wound that never healed, causing so bad an odor that nuns shunned her. She died in May 1457. After her death, the convent needed money to pay its bills; the superior prayed for her intercession. Not long after, the nuns found the needed amount of money in the alms box. When the nuns needed wine for their meals, they appealed to her, and shortly after, a man appeared at the door with a barrel of wine. Her body was kept in a glass reliquary and was observed to turn to face the people; sometimes, her eyes moved. One day, fire broke out in a home; a piece of her relic was thrown into the fire, and the fire was immediately extinguished. Many more miracles were reported as a result of her intercession. She was canonized by Leo XIII in 1900 (*ES*).

Lessons on obedience and humility, prayer, honesty, devotion to the mother of Christ, spreading the kingdom of God, intimacy with God through meditation and prayer, love for the Holy Eucharist, compassion for captives, resistance to temptations, and avoidance of occasions of sin—these are Christ's teachings exemplified by the Saints through miracles.

They Braved Fires

St. John the Evangelist converted Polycarp to Christianity and later appointed him bishop of Smyrna. Under Marcus Aurelius, a persecution arose, and *St. Polycarp* was brought to the proconsul.

NICHOLAS LLANES ROSAL, STD, PHL, MSJ

Threatened to be thrown into a den of wild beasts if he did not blaspheme Christ, he said, "I have served Him these fourscore and six years, and He never did me any harm, but much good. How can I blaspheme my King and my Savior?" Promising to burn him, the proconsul continued to force him to renounce his Christian faith, to which the Saint said, "You threaten with fire which burns for a short time and then goes out. But you don't know the judgment to come and the fire of everlasting torments which is prepared for the wicked. Why do you delay?" Soldiers set fire on a heap of wood around him, but the fire left him unharmed. The soldiers then pierced his heart, and Christians carried his body away to be buried (*ES*).

After she was converted by St. Paul in Iconium, eighteen-year-old *St. Thecla* left her fiancé, a pagan. Threatened with fire if she did not renounce her faith, she made the sign of the cross and flung herself into the fire that had been prepared for her. Suddenly, a downpour came and extinguished the fire. She left for Antioch. Persecuted because of her faith in Jesus, she was thrown to the wild beasts. Angry that she was alive, soldiers "bound her to bulls they drove in different directions." Still unharmed, they cast her into a pit of serpents. By the grace of God, she came out alive. She returned to her native country and devoted her life to works of kindness, performing many miracles until she died at age ninety (*HF*).

Valerian and his brother *Tiburtius* agreed to convert to Christianity and be baptized if they could see *St. Cecilia's* guardian angel. Instructed and baptized, they were ecstatic when they saw the radiant angel by the side of the Saint as she knelt in prayer. Because of their faith, the brothers were arrested and thrown into a heap of burning wood. Surviving, they were beheaded on orders of the prefect Almachius. Pursuing the properties of the brothers, Almachius found out that Cecilia, who married Valerian after his baptism, had given away everything to the poor. Incensed, the prefect ordered Cecilia to be tortured day and night by the heat of the bath in her own house. When she was found unhurt, an executioner went with an ax to cut her head off. Unable to finish the job with three strokes, the executioner left her half-dead until she passed away three days later (*HF*).

Blessed Margaret of Costello's deformity embarrassed her parents. She was a hunchbacked dwarf who was blind and lame. Going to the healing shrine of the Città di Castello, her parents sought a miracle. When none came, they brought her to a parish church and abandoned her there. One compassionate family after another and nuns in a local convent took her in. She finally settled in a foster home. Nurturing her spiritual life with prayer and suffering, she became a devout Dominican tertiary. In one of those homes where she was staying, fire broke out. Climbing up to the top of the stairs, she took off her mantle and threw it to the firefighters, telling them to throw it into the fire. The fire instantly went out (*ES*).

At a public debate about the divinity of Christ between the Albigenses and *St. Dominic,* the panel of judges could not tell who won. They agreed to decide the outcome with a trial by fire. They threw the heretics' thesis into the fire, and the document was consumed immediately. They threw St. Dominic's, and it flew into the air unscathed. They threw it two more times, and the result was the same. On another occasion, St. Dominic lodged at a poor woman's home where he exchanged his hair shirt for a coarser one. After he was gone, the home burned down, but the box containing his hair shirt was found untouched by the fire (*HF/ES*).

They Stopped Earthquakes, Even Caused a Storm

Once a year, St. Benedict made it a point to visit his sister, *St. Scholastica,* in her convent five miles lower down the mountain from his Monte Cassino monastery. On his last visit, St. Scholastica, who always loved praying together and conversing with him about God, urged him to stay until the following morning. Hearing an obstinate denial to her request, St. Scholastica prayed to God to intervene. No sooner after saying "Amen" to her prayer, a violent storm came, preventing St. Benedict from leaving. Complaining, he told her, "God forgive you, Sister. What have you done?" They spent the whole night talking again about God and the happiness of souls in heaven. Three days later, St. Benedict, in contemplation, saw his sister's soul in the form of a dove fly to heaven (*HF*).

In 1645, Quito, Ecuador, was visited by frequent earthquakes that resulted in diseases and many deaths. The disasters prompted a priest to say that he would gladly give his life to stop these misfortunes. Hearing this comment, *St. Mariana de Jesus de Quito,* a devotee of the Blessed Virgin, told the priest that his life was too precious. She would rather give her life in place of the priest's. Shortly after, she became very ill and died. The earthquakes stopped, and the epidemic ceased. This was one among her miracles that proved her sanctity from an early age. Orphaned at age four, Mariana went to live with her older sister and grew up helping the poor, doing penance, and teaching Indian children in the small hut she had built behind her sister's home. She often wore a crown of thorns to remind herself of the sufferings of Jesus and of her own death. She passed away at age twenty-seven, was beatified in 1959 by Pope John XXIII, and canonized by Pope John Paul II in 1990 (*ES*).

One night, a busload of pilgrims on their way to San Giovanni Rotondo, where *Padre Pio* lived, met an intense lightning storm in the Apennine Mountains. Having been advised by the Saint to seek the help of their guardian angels to ask help from the Saint's guardian angel, they did just that. The following morning, before the pilgrims could tell their story, Padre Pio told them he had been awakened by his guardian angel to pray for them (*ES*). Wow! Guardian angels talk to and help one another!

They Defied the Enemies of God

When Attila the Hun, called the Scourge of God, was approaching Rome after plundering Milan and Pavia, the citizens pleaded with *St. Leo the Great* to go meet him. "Contrary to expectations, Attila received the Pope with great honor." According to tradition, Attila saw the pope flanked by two venerable-looking men, believed to be Sts. Peter and Paul, as the pope stood before the Hun. Another tradition says that Attila saw St. Michael behind St. Leo with a threatening look. The Hun agreed to accept an annual tribute in exchange for leaving Rome. However, North African Vandals—not the Huns—sacked the city the following year, carrying captives away with them. They later allowed the pope to send missionary priests to purchase the captives' freedom (*ES*).

Although very ill, *St. Clare,* founder of the Franciscan Poor Clare, allowed herself to be carried with the Blessed Sacrament to the wall of the city where the invading Saracens could see it. She went down on her knees and prayed to God to save her convent from attack, saying, "Lord, protect these Sisters whom I cannot protect now." A voice answered, "I will keep them always in my care." Instantly, the attackers fled (*ES*).

A woman who did not believe in the host as the body of Christ baked bread. *St. Gregory the Great* placed the bread on the altar, and it began to bleed. An Albigensian heretic challenged *St. Anthony* to prove the presence of Christ in the Blessed Sacrament. The dare: if a mule that hadn't eaten for three days bowed before the Eucharist, he would believe. The mule was given hay but refused to touch it. Instead, the mule knelt and bowed before the Blessed Sacrament (*HF/ES*).

Publicly professing their Christian faith in Rome where they lived, husband and wife *Chrysanthus* and *Daria* instructed and led many people to be baptized. When Celestinus heard about this, he ordered his tribune to arrest them. Chrysanthus was chained, but the chains broke. He was wrapped in ox skin and exposed to the burning sun, fettered again, and then thrown into a dungeon. Again, the chains broke, and the prison shone with a dazzling light. Meanwhile, Daria was dragged into a brothel, but a lion protected her from harm. Finally, both were thrown into a pit, and soldiers rained stones on them (*HF*).

During the reign of Diocletian, *St. Januarius,* bishop of Benevento, Italy, went to visit Christian prisoners Sosius and Proculus in Pozzuoli. When the district governor Timothy found that out, St. Januarius and the prisoners were brought before him and were ordered to carry loads of iron on their shoulders and walk in front of the governor's chariot on its way to the amphitheater. With others who were awaiting execution, they were dragged to the amphitheater where wild animals roamed. When no one was harmed, the people said it was due to magic. Executioners then beheaded them (*ES*).

In the year 400, St. Januarius' relics were taken to Naples, where he was proclaimed patron of the city. The people attributed to him their deliverance from plague in 1407 and from disasters caused by Mount Vesuvius. Since the transfer of his relics to Naples, three times a year (Sept. 19, Dec. 10, and first Sunday of May) with rare exceptions, a sealed phial containing the congealed blood of St. Januarius, when placed near his head, liquefies and bubbles up.

They Cured the Sick

St. Blaise studied philosophy but later became a physician. Witnessing so much misery among the poor amid the abuses of the rich, he became a priest and later was made bishop. Arrested for his Christian faith, he was on his way to prison when a distraught mother carrying her child dying of throat disease threw him at his feet. Moved by the mother's faith, he touched the child, and the child was cured. Since then, St. Blaise became known as the patron saint of people suffering from throat disease. The church celebrates his feast on February 3 and offers a special blessing of the throat on that day (*HF*/*ES*).

She was a rich, beautiful thirteen-year-old Roman girl whom young noblemen vied to marry. Refusing to consider any of them, she was accused of being a Christian. The judge made her all kinds of promises to sway her away from her Christian faith. Courageously professing that she had no other desire but to be a spouse of Jesus Christ, *St. Agnes* was ordered by the judge to be dragged before the idols and forced to offer incense. Defying the judge, she made the sign of the cross instead. They took her to a house of ill repute, but she told the executioners, "You may stain your sword with my blood, but you will never be able to profane my body. I have consecrated it to Christ." She became stiff like a statue, and the soldiers could not move her. A young man approached to touch her. In an instant, a flash of lightning struck him blind, and he fell trembling to the ground. His friends carried him to St. Agnes, who had now left the scene, singing the praises of the Lord. Through her prayer, the young man's sight was restored (*HF*).

St. John Nepomucene was ordered by King Wenceslas to be tortured then killed for refusing to reveal Queen Sophie's confession. At night, his body was thrown into the river, which was lit by a bright light. In response to the Prague Army's prayers, he appeared to the soldiers on the eve of battle, and they won the battle and saved the city and Bavaria from their enemies. He was also credited for saving the town of Nepomuk from bubonic plague. Cardinal Michael Althan, viceroy of Naples, was cured of his paralysis the moment he invoked the name of St. John Nepomucene. He was canonized around 1721 (*ES*).

In 1875, *St. Katherine Drexel* (born in Philadelphia, Pennsylvania, on Nov. 30, 1848) and her sisters inherited $14 million (a billion in the twenty-first century) in a trust fund from their father, a railroad tycoon and Philadelphia banker. The money generated an annual income of $400,000. She used her share to build and support schools and missions for Native and African Americans. When she asked Leo XIII to send more priests to Wyoming, the pope asked her to become a missionary herself. At that, in 1889, she entered the novitiate of the Sisters of Mercy and, in 1891, started the Sisters of the Blessed Sacrament for Indians and Colored People. With the help of St. Frances Cabrini, the new congregation of nuns was approved by the Vatican. She built missions in different states and, in 1925, founded New Orleans' Xavier University for minorities to help train teachers. By 1942, she had forty mission centers, fifty Indian missions, black Catholic schools in thirteen states, and twenty-three rural schools (*ES*).

On March 3, 1955, the Saint who had practiced self-flagellation and austerity in the midst of her wealthy environment died of natural causes at the age of ninety-six. A crypt containing her body is kept in the congregation's motherhouse in Bethlehem, Pennsylvania. More than four thousand people attribute miraculous cures to her. The cure of a seventeen-month-old boy with nerve deafness and a deaf seven-year-old girl were declared miracles by the Vatican as results of her intercession. Beatified in 1988 by Pope John Paul II, she was canonized on Oct. 1, 2000, by the same pope. St. Katherine is the second American-born Saint after St. Elizabeth Ann Seton.

In 312, when her son, Emperor Constantine, was in the battlefield, a cross appeared in the sky, and below it were the words "In hoc signo vinces" (By this sign thou shalt conquer). He converted to Christianity, and soon after, his mother, Empress Helena, became a Christian as well. The emperor's conversion resulted in the freedom of Christians to practice their faith openly. Inspired by the apparition of the cross and the sign below it, *St. Helena* decided to pursue her desire to find the cross of the Redeemer. At age eighty (according to one writer), she traveled to Jerusalem. Finding three crosses, she, with unwavering faith, asked a sick person to come forward and have the cross touch him. The third try resulted in a cure. On the spot where she found the cross, she had the Basilica of the Holy Cross built and, on September 15, 335, placed a large piece of the cross in a rich silver shrine. Another piece was brought by a knight crusader to France. (Many churches and individuals claim to have small pieces of the cross in their possession. One of this writer's theology professors commented that if all those chips and pieces from the holy cross were gathered together today, they would make a whole forest! Possible? Can't tell for sure, but if you think of the multiplication of bread in the desert as a real miracle, could those claims be far from reality?) That day was promulgated in the fifth century as the Feast of the Exaltation of the Holy Cross to be celebrated every year by the Roman and Eastern Churches (*HF*).

Influenced by St. Alphonsus Rodriguez, *St. Peter Claver* became a Jesuit. Ordained as a priest in 1616, St. Peter sought to dedicate himself to missionary work in Colombia where Cartagena, its largest city, was the center of slave trade in South America. The plight of bonded Africans who arrived there by the hundreds caused in him a lot of pain. It prompted him to minister to them, begging food to give them, washing their wounds, burying their dead, and with the help of an interpreter, teaching them about Christ. It's said that he baptized over three hundred thousand slaves, including infants. He preached and heard confessions in the city and in the hinterlands. He fought for laws to protect their Christian marriages and the unity of their families. He frequented hospitals where he was sometimes seen as an angel. His cloak he used to cover lepers; touching it, the sick were said to be cured. Victim of the plague that struck Cartagena in 1650, he became bedridden for four years and was practically forgotten. When he died, people went to his cell, taking anything they could carry for relics. He was canonized by Leo XIII in 1888 (*ES*).

They Levitated and Shone

Christ's ascension to heaven was a celebration of Christ's victory over the world, as He told His apostles (Jn 16:10-11). Rising above the earth into His Father's abode was His reward for conquering sin and death. By dying to sin and earthly allures, the Saints also rise, elevating themselves to the world of the spirit. For their prize, they are sometimes given by God the privilege to enjoy visions of Christ, angels, and saints; they even experience heaven while yet living in the world. Many of them have ecstasies that give them a glimpse of what they forever will experience in the next life. Among the living, they are seen at times to shine like the noon sun or radiant angels. They have been observed to rise above the ground a foot or higher as they are praying or in contemplation. These are men and women who live in the real world yet are detached from its deceitful promises.

Those are Saints who have been recognized for their heroic sanctity, like *St. Ignatius of Loyola*, founder of the Jesuit Order. As a manifestation of his holy life, he was seen many times elevated

NICHOLAS LLANES ROSAL, STD, PHL, MSJ

and radiant as he prayed—a reward here on earth for his deep love of God and remarkable apostolic work. He brought different ethnic groups, including Jews, into the faith. He reformed lives of sinners (among them, loose women), evangelized distant mission regions of the world, and advocated education on all levels. The *Spiritual Exercises* he wrote and spread is a mirror of his deep spirituality that reflects his extraordinary way of communicating with God and of living the virtues of love of neighbor, chastity, poverty, and obedience. Mirroring his spirit today are thousands of Jesuit priests and brothers working in every apostolic field in practically every nation of the world. Among St. Ignatius' sons is Francis I, the first Jesuit pope in the history of the church (*ES*).

Santa Teresa of Avila was another Saint who was seen several times to levitate and "bathed in rays of brilliant gold while writing at her desk." A contemplative, she wrote several books on spirituality that describe how a soul can ascend to the highest level of perfection. In her books *Life*, *The Way to Perfection*, and *The Interior Castle*, she explains that one can reach, step-by-step, the highest level of perfection where God practically works in the soul alone because here, after going through a "dark night" of suffering, purification, and illumination, the soul reaches an intimate union with God. At that point, the soul, ever resigned and docile to God's will, can say, "Nada te turbe, Solo Dios basta" (Let nothing disturb you. Only God suffices).

One can have a glimpse of the intimacy between Sta. Teresa and Jesus from a conversation between them when she was suffering terribly from poor health after founding her seventeenth monastery. She complained, and Jesus told her, "Teresa, so do I treat my friends." Known for her strong character, she retorted, "That's why you have so few friends!" Who can dare talk like that except one in deep intimacy with her friend? (This writer was fortunate for having seen the visitors' parlor in Santa Teresa's Avila convent where she had a vision of "Jesus being tied to the pillar bleeding." That vision converted her from worldliness to the spirituality that took her to the highest level of perfection. This writer also saw the Saint's dormitory room in the same convent where Jesus as a child appeared to her after her night prayers. At this surprise visit by Jesus, an exchange of sweet pleasantries took place. Jesus asked her, "Who are you?" Santa Teresa replied, "I am Teresa of Jesus. And who are you?" Child Jesus answered, "I am Jesus of Teresa") (*ES*).

Sta. Teresa had a Carmelite priest for a confessor, a Saint—*John of the Cross*—whom she affectionately called Medio Fraile (a half Friar) because he stood just a wee bit taller than a midget. (This writer saw in her Avila convent a child's chair where St. John used to sit to hear the confessions of Sta. Teresa and her nuns.) On the urging of Sta. Teresa, he founded the Discalced Order of Carmelites, an order whose members walked barefoot as penitential practice; they were allowed later to wear sandals. Seeing the sad laxity in both the Carmelite friars' and nuns' convents, Sta. Teresa and St. John agreed to work together to reform them by enforcing the rules of the Carmelite Order: spirituality, devotion to the Blessed Sacrament, prayer, meditation, penance, and a disciplined practice of the vows of poverty, chastity, and obedience. Sta. Teresa took charge of reforming the nuns' convents; St. John, the men's convents.

St. John suffered persecution for his reform work. Kidnapped by the unreformed Carmelites, he was kept for nine months in a dark cell where he had to stand on a stool to reach the light from a small window to pray his hours. On two occasions, eyewitnesses saw brilliant light emanating from his cell; the light vanished when they entered. He was whipped every evening, then three times a week, and later, Fridays only. He was ordered to eat a beggar's meal, sitting on the floor, and after the meal, the friars would pass by him, hitting him on the head. According to tradition, the Blessed Virgin helped him escape by loosening the lock on his cell window, allowing him to climb down, walk to a nuns' convent, and hide in the infirmary (*ES*).

St. John's spirituality is described in his books *The Ascent of Mount Carmel*, *The Living Flame of Love*, and *The Dark Night of the Soul*. In those works, he describes how a soul goes through three successive ways to achieve perfect unity with God: the *purgative* way, whereby God comes down on the soul with trials and sufferings to purify it; the *illuminative* way, by which man is inspired by God with contemplation and understanding of His mystical messages; and the *unitive* way, which leads to an intimate union with God. He wrote poems that were counted among the best literary works in Spanish. When St. John of the Cross died, light "like the sun, moon, and stars together" shone above his bed, a similar phenomenon eyewitnesses had seen around him on many occasions.

St. Benedict Joseph Labre, oldest of eighteen children, studied under his uncle, a priest, for six years. After the uncle's death, the Saint attempted to enter the Trappist and Cistercian orders but was rejected. He became a pilgrim, visiting European shrines and begging for food. When none would give him any, he would rummage through garbage heaps. Faithful to the Blessed Sacrament, he spent hours praying in church, never failing to attend the Forty Hours devotion. In the Church of the Gesù in Rome, he was frequently observed having ecstasies and seen lifted from the ground as he prayed. He collapsed at the steps of the Church of Santa Maria del Monti in Rome and died. After his death, his biographer (Marconi, his confessor) documented 136 miracles. He was canonized in 1883 by Leo XIII and proclaimed patron saint of beggars (*ES*).

According to his biographers, *St. Jean-Baptiste-Marie Vianney* practiced severe mortification for more than forty years. He experienced several mystical experiences, including receiving a gold ring he wore to signify his "mystical marriage" with Christ. Many people who went to him for confession *saw brilliant light radiating from the confessional.* Although he hardly passed the examinations required before his ordination, his unction as a homilist and holy life as a confessor brought pilgrims to him from countries outside France, including countries from Asia. (This writer personally knew a saintly Philippine archbishop, now deceased, who traveled to Ars to kneel at the Saint's side to confess. He had also gone to San Giovanni Rotondo monastery in Italy to make his confession to Padre Pio.) The Saint wrote most of his fiery sermons because of poor memory. Most of those sermons have been destroyed. Criticized by his peers because of his lowly family background (he grew up as a shepherd in a farm in Dardilly) and poor academic record, St. John suffered humiliations that he bore patiently and charitably. He was canonized by Pope Pius XI in 1925 and proclaimed patron saint of parish priests (*HF/ES*).

Many more Saints were recorded to have been seen lifted from the ground as they prayed or meditated, radiating light that reflected Jesus' transfiguration. These were Saints like *St. Philip Neri*, founder of the Confraternity of the Most Holy Trinity, whose ecstasies were so deep people thought he was dying. He could read minds. He told a young man once that not a word of his confession contained truth. He converted a nobleman by showing him a vision of hell. He fell very ill one day and was on the verge of death when he was found raised a foot above his bed with his arms spread out as if he was in an embrace with someone. He recovered and revealed that Mary had appeared to him and healed him. He was canonized by Pope Gregory XV in 1622 (*ES*).

St. Anthony Mary Claret, founder of the Claretian Order, the Missionary Sons of the Immaculate Heart of Mary, dedicated himself to apostolic work in Catalonia, Spain, and in the Canary Islands. Named archbishop of Santiago, Cuba, he worked there for a few years but met opposition that prompted him to go back to Spain. He became confessor of the queen and accompanied her on her exile to France. While deep in prayer, he was seen to levitate to as high as two feet. His passionate devotion to the Blessed Virgin brought him ecstasies, exuding and diffusing bodily heat around people near him. Claretian missionaries today work in many countries, including the United States and the Philippines. He was canonized by Pius XII in 1950 (*ES*).

St. Gerard Majella was seen in various places multiplying food for the poor as he was at the same time in church, levitating and falling into ecstasies. *St. Francis of Paola*, founder of the Minim

Friars (from the word *minimum*, "least," to express a life of humility), was seen simultaneously working in the kitchen or preaching on the streets while at the altar praying, levitating and in ecstasy. *St. Anthony of Padua* had numerous ecstasies. In one instance, very bright light was observed emanating from his room, and when he was watched through a small opening in his door, he was seen to be carrying the young child Jesus in his arms (*HF/ES*).

The son of Juan de Porres, a Spanish knight, and a freed slave, *St. Martin de Porres* was baptized by the same priest as St. Rose of Lima, Peru. He and his sister grew up in the care of his mother. The father provided them with a tutor when he brought them with him briefly in Ecuador. Back in Lima, St. Martin lived an austere life, spending hours in prayer and penance. He learned to be a barber, a well-paying job that involved some herbal healing and surgery. Joining the Third Order of St. Dominic, he performed lowly tasks as a lay brother and became known as the Saint of the Broom. He lived an austere life, spending hours in prayer and penance, even flogging himself until he bled. He was observed to levitate and radiate bright light many times and rise to kiss the crucifix hanging on the church wall.

Devils used to accost him, even setting his cell on fire. He collected alms, increasing them miraculously and giving them to the poor. He ministered to the sick regardless of their station in life. While in Peru performing the menial tasks assigned to him, he was seen in Mexico, China, Japan, and the Philippines, doing works of charity. Curing a lot of people, he was called to minister to the archbishop of Peru and the Spanish viceroy, both having fallen seriously ill. Before his death, St. Martin was visited by the devil again, this time praising him to make him feel vain. But the Blessed Virgin, St. Dominic, and St. Vincent appeared and drove the devil away. After he died, people approached his coffin, tearing pieces off his habit for relics. The friars had to replace his habit three times. Countless people have reported favors because of his intercession. He was canonized in 1962 by Pope John XXIII (*HF/ES*).

They Received the Gift of Tongues

Born to a noble family in Valencia, Spain, Vincent became a Dominican when he was seventeen. Soon after he finished his studies in Barcelona, he taught in Lerida, having among his students Pierre Fouloup, who became the grand inquisitor of Aragon. Vincent was appointed by Cardinal Pedro de Luna (who later became Antipope Benedict XIII) as his confessor and apostolic penitentiary. He was offered an appointment as cardinal, but he refused, preferring to dedicate his life to preaching. Becoming very ill, he had a vision of Christ, St. Dominic, and St. Francis of Assisi, who told him to go out and preach, and he recovered and went out preaching penance. Although he spoke only his native dialect, *St. Vincent Ferrer* was understood by his foreign audiences. According to tradition, *St. Vincent had the gift of bilocation*. While in Europe preaching, he was also seen distributing food among children in Northern Africa. He was known to be constantly fasting and living an austere life. He was canonized in 1455. To date, many favors have been reported due to his intercession (*HF/ES*).

St. Anthony of Padua's gift of tongues touched many groups of people—from the poor to the clergy and hierarchy to the heretics and public officials. On one occasion when no speaker for an ordination ceremony was found, in desperation, St. Anthony's superior commanded him to go to the pulpit and speak whatever the Holy Spirit prompted him to say. Unable to refuse, he preached to the amazement of his audience (Dominicans, Franciscans, and public officials) with such eloquence, wisdom, and unction that the provincial took him out of his permanent kitchen assignment and commanded him to preach throughout Lombardy. In addition, St. Francis appointed him to teach theology to Franciscans. His preaching and debates with Albigenses earned him the title Hammer of Heretics. After his canonization, St. Anthony's tomb was opened, and the friars found his tongue incorrupt. St. Bonaventure kissed it and reminded the world of the Saint's special gift from the Holy Spirit—the gift of tongues (*ES*).

NICHOLAS LLANES ROSAL, STD, PHL, MSJ

Among countless other Saints who were given the gift of tongues were St. Stephen, the Evangelist St. Luke, the early disciples, and countless martyrs. Among latter Saints were St. Ambrose, St. Augustine, St. Benedict, St. Dominic, St. Ignatius, St. Francis of Assisi, St. John Vianney, St. Gerald, St. Vincent Ferrer, St. Anthony of Egypt, St. Anthony Claret, St. Teresa of Avila, St. Catherine of Siena, St. Philip Neri, St. Thomas Aquinas, St. Hyacinth, St. Francis Xavier, St. Peter Claver, and many more.

There were Saints, though illiterate or hardly educated, who were inspired by the Holy Spirit to spread the word of God. Such was *St. Benedict the Moor*, whose parents were black slaves brought in chains from Africa to Sicily. Impressing the village people with his sincerity and hard work, he was given his freedom at age eighteen. With his small earnings, he helped the poor and the sick, a life of virtue that earned him the title Holy Negro. However, there were people who ridiculed him for his love of neighbor and his skin color. One day, a nobleman heard people insulting St. Benedict. Stopping to defend him, Jerome Lanza, a man who had renounced the world and gone to live in the hills as a hermit, said, "You are making fun of this poor Negro now, but in a few years, his name will be famous." St. Benedict joined Jerome's group of hermits and, upon Lanza's death, was chosen leader. Urged by Pius IV to join religious orders, the hermits did so, and Benedict became a lay brother in the Order of Friars Minor. He excelled in the love of the Blessed Sacrament and the Blessed Virgin, living a life of humility and meekness. His reputation as a holy person spread, and people, including the archbishop of Palermo and the viceroy of Sicily, sought his counsel. In 1578, the friars chose this illiterate brother to be the superior of the priory. "Although unable to read, he was able to explain the Holy Scripture and the teachings of the Church with clarity." When his tenure as superior was over, he asked to return to his former assignment as priory cook. He foretold the hour and day of his death; he passed away on April 4, 1589. He was canonized in 1807 by Pius VII. His body was kept in a shrine provided by Philip III of Spain (*HF*).

Other Saints who were sought for their holiness and wisdom though hardly literate were *St. Alphonsus Rodriguez*—a Jesuit brother who guided many people, including *St. Peter Claver* before St. Peter could decide what to do with his vocation (*HF*)—and *St. Labre*, the patron of beggars (*ES*). These humble men lived exemplary holy lives with their extraordinary love for God and neighbor, according to the words of St. Paul: "Charity edifies" (1 Cor 8:2).

ESSAY 5

They Saw Jesus

*S*T. *MARGARET MARY Alacoque,* born in 1647 in the Burgundy Valley of France, practiced mortification so severely at age nine that she fell ill with rheumatic fever, causing her to spend four years paralyzed in bed. At age fifteen, she was cured instantly when she promised the Virgin Mary that she would consecrate herself a virgin and enter a religious order. One day, after communion, she saw Jesus as "the most handsome, richest, and most powerful" man. The vision prompted her to renew her promise to the Blessed Virgin and to dedicate her entire self to Jesus. At age seventeen, after she and her brother (who eventually became a priest) attended a carnival party, she had a vision of the scourging of Christ, who reproached her for her unfaithfulness. She wept bitterly. At age twenty-four, she entered the Visitation Convent. Then, Jesus, for a year and a half, repeatedly appeared to her, calling her the Beloved Disciple of the Sacred Heart. In her autobiography, St. Margaret describes the Sacred Heart as "a resplendent sun, the burning rays of which fell vertically upon my heart, which was inflamed with a fire so fervid that it seemed as if it would reduce me to ashes."

Jesus taught her the devotions that would become known as the Nine Fridays and the Holy Hour. He also asked her to promote the Feast of the Sacred Heart on the Friday after the octave of the feast of Corpus Christi. Inspired by Jesus, she started to pray while lying prostrate with her face to the ground from 11:00 p.m. to midnight on the eve of the first Friday of each month to make amends for the apostles' abandonment of Jesus during His passion. Her visions earned her ridicule from her superior and peers. However, the Jesuit father Claude La Colombière, the convent confessor, supported her, and a team of theologians accepted the visions as genuine. A new superior came in, and in 1688, a chapel was built at Paray-le-Monial. The devotion to the Sacred Heart and the first-Friday devotion spread to other Visitation convents and the rest of the world. The devotion was designed to manifest the believers' desire to repair the world's ingratitude to Jesus' love and to show their faith in the Sacred Heart's compassion to grant them the gift of a happy death and eternal salvation. St. Margaret Mary was canonized by Benedict XV in 1864 (*HF/ES*).

When he was growing up in Assisi, *Francis* spent his life with friends, drinking and extravagantly spending his rich father's money. During a war that broke out between his city and neighboring Perugia, he joined his city's military and was captured. Ransomed after a year, Francis soon responded to a call for knights for the Fourth Crusade. He sported his shining armor and rich garments and bragged he would return a prince. However, not gone very far from Assisi, he met a gentleman and traded his fine clothes and armor with the man's rags. He fell ill and heard a voice telling him to go home and serve God instead of "serving the man." He did and started visiting the sick and helping the poor. Praying and crying over his sins in a cave, he decided to visit the abandoned church of San Damiano where he heard a voice from the crucifix, telling him three times, "Francis, repair my house which you see falling down." He went home, took one of his father's horses and a lot of cloth, sold them, and then rebuilt the church. His father went to the church to take him home, but Francis hid. After praying and fasting, he came out of hiding and was confronted by his father. Unable to persuade his son to get rid of his "insane" ideas, the father demanded that he either come home or renounce his inheritance and repay the cost of the horse and cloth. Francis surprised him by taking off all his clothing and giving them to him. He renounced his patrimony and made a vow of absolute poverty.

NICHOLAS LLANES ROSAL, STD, PHL, MSJ

Nothing on his back but laborer's clothing given him by a sympathizer, *St. Francis* went out and gathered twelve followers. Clothed in rough woolen habits and rough tunics and carrying neither gold nor silver, they went begging and preaching as itinerants. The group grew larger and became a religious order for which he wrote the rules based on the gospels to ensure discipline and achieve the organization's spiritual purpose—sanctification of its members through prayer, penance, and exemplary observance of poverty, chastity, and obedience. The rules were approved verbally by Pope Innocent III in 1210 and formally in 1223. St. Francis' and his followers' preaching covered a wide area, including such Muslim countries as Syria and Egypt. He even met with a Muslim head of state. His planned mission among Muslims in 1212 ended in a shipwreck and illness. The group's spirit spread very quickly, attracting so many followers that by the time the General Chapter took place in 1219, the order was said to have as many as five thousand members. On September 14, 1224, the Feast of the Exaltation of the Holy Cross, he was in ecstasy, "meditating on the passion of Christ when a seraph appeared with six fiery wings descending from heaven." In the fold of the wings, the crucified Jesus appeared. When the vision ended, he found his hands and feet with black naillike outgrowths and saw a wound on his side oozing with blood. For two years, St. Francis would try to hide these stigmata, but his friars would discover them from the way he walked (he limped badly) and from bloodstains on his habit. They also witnessed him perform miracles, multiplying food, influencing the weather, and subduing fierce animals but befriending and preaching to birds and fishes. Nearing death, he broke bread with his disciples, asked them to sing the "Canticle of Brother Sun" he had composed, blessed his brothers, and then expired. The date was October 4, 1225. He was canonized by Pope Gregory IX in 1228 (*HF/ES*).

St. Catherine of Siena, one of the four female doctors of the church (St. Teresa of Avila, St. Therese of Lisieux, and St. Hildegard of Bingen, a Benedictine abbess [declared last 2012 as a doctor by Benedict XVI]), was a mystic who was commanded by Jesus to go out into the world to help the church during an upheaval about the papacy and a war between the Papal States and Rome. When Catherine, the youngest in a family of twenty-five children, was six, she had a vision of Christ in pontifical robes and wearing a tiara while with Sts. Peter and Paul and St. John the Evangelist atop the Church of St. Dominic. As young as she was, she wore a hair shirt that kept her aware continually of the sufferings of Christ. At age seven, she made a vow of virginity and, at sixteen, donned the Dominican habit as a tertiary. As she grew up, Jesus continued to appear to her and talked to her through her inner voice. When she turned nineteen, she saw Jesus with the Blessed Virgin Mary, St. John the Evangelist, St. Dominic, and David. Jesus spoke to her, asking her to accept Him as her spouse in faith. He extended His hand to slip an exquisite ring into Catherine's right-hand finger as King David played the harp in celebration. The heavenly nuptial ring would always be seen by her but invisible to others (*ES*). (Among other Saints who received the divine nuptial ring were St. Teresa of Avila and St. John Vianney.)

St. Catherine of Siena received other mystical gifts, like levitating and emitting light. She multiplied bread, healed the sick, and could smell the stench of sin in others. She was reported to have raised her mother from the dead. Illiterate until she reached adult age, she was taught by the Holy Spirit to read and write. She wrote the *Dialogue*, a book about her mystical experiences; wrote four hundred letters to counsel the popes, the clergy, the public officials, and the people who sought advice from her; and wrote a collection of prayers. Her Italian writing style was acclaimed as highly classical. Known to Pope Gregory XI, she was consulted about the crusade against the Turks, the reformation of the clergy, and the administration of Holy See affairs. She became a peace ambassador between Florence and Rome and between the pope and Clement VII (the antipope) and stood by Urban VI, who ascended to the papacy following the death of Gregory XI. From her deathbed, she reconciled Pope Urban VI and the Roman Republic. She died at age thirty-three on April 29, 1380. Many of her relics were distributed among various convents in Europe, including the

Dominican Sisters' Convent in Rome and a Dominican convent in England. Many miraculous favors, particularly involving the sick, have been reported due to her intercession.

Padre Pio was born in Pietrelcina, a farming town in Southern Italy. Although suffering from tuberculosis, he was ordained a Capuchin priest and called into the army during World War I. He served only for two years due to poor health. Continuing to suffer from his poor health, he was assigned to the monastery of San Giovanni Rotondo, where he lived until he died. One day, he started experiencing intermittent half-inch bloodless wounds in his palms, an experience that went on for eight years. One day in 1918, while hearing the confession of a young boy, an "angel appeared holding a long, sharp steel knife that he hurled into the Saint's soul," causing an intense pain. A month later, kneeling before a large crucifix, he received the stigmata that continuously bled, forcing him to use gloves except when saying mass. The stigmata would continue until the time he predicted they would heal, which was on the day of his death. Doctors had examined the wounds but could not explain any natural cause. His tuberculosis disappeared. He was forbidden to preach but allowed to say mass and hear confession, drawing people from various countries, including the Philippines (*ES*).

He established the Home for the Relief of Suffering and a hospital. He was known to bilocate. As yet a seminarian, he was in the choir when he suddenly found himself in a distant home where a child was being born and the father was dying. The mother saw the Capuchin in the room. A girl was born, then the husband died. Years later, Padre Pio heard the daughter's confession then disappeared from the confessional. She found him at the Rotondo and became a devout follower. People who sought his intercession must talk to their guardian angels to talk to his guardian angel if they wanted favors from him. His guardian angel helped him understand foreign languages, especially at the confessional. Padre Pio died on January 23, 1968, was beatified by Pope John Paul II on May 2, 1999, and was canonized by him in 2002.

When *St. Gemma Galgani* was nineteen, she turned down two marriage proposals. Born in Tuscany, she wanted to become a Passionist nun but was denied admission because of poor health. Falling seriously ill with meningitis, she turned to Venerable Francis Possenti (later canonized as St. Gabriel Francis of Our Lady of Sorrows) and was cured. Her devotion to the Blessed Virgin moved her to repent her sins, to do penance, and to desire sufferings for the sake of Jesus' mother. Her guardian angel and the Blessed Mother appeared to her. Opening her mantle and covering her with it, Mary told her of her Son's love of her. Soon, Jesus appeared with his open wounds. From them, flames, not blood, darted into her hands, feet, and heart, causing her unbearable pain. When the vision ended, she found herself on her knees unable to move, whereby her angel helped her to bed. Blood began to flow from the wounds. Every Thursday evening into Friday afternoon, she would experience ecstasy as the wounds would open and issue blood. When the rapture ended, the wounds would close, leaving only white scars. Father Germano, a Passionist priest and her spiritual director, sent her to a family to work as a mother's helper, a job that shielded her from exposure to the public. The priest tested her and found her mystic experiences to be genuine. Nevertheless, he told her to stop accepting the stigmata and urged her to help the poor and pray for the conversion of sinners. The stigmatic experiences stopped, but the white marks stayed (*HF/ES*).

St. Gemma had a very special relationship with her guardian angel. Falling into ecstasies, the Saint saw her angel frequently and would carry on a two-way conversation. People around them would hear only Saint Gemma speak, but the angel would be there. Twice Father Germano was among people who witnessed those conversations. But while the angel treated her like she was her sister, the devils persistently tempted her, even hitting her with blows on the shoulders, especially when she was praying. Sometimes, the angel would excuse herself, leaving her alone for the whole night, saying she also had to sleep. Gemma would tell her, "Angels of Jesus don't sleep." The angel would say that angels needed rest too. The Saint's angel served as her courier, bringing letters back and forth between her and Father Germano and her relatives. Other angels used to visit St. Gemma. When she was distracted in prayer, the angels would nudge her. She was seen levitating many times and kissing the crucifix on a wall, like St. Martin de Porres. She knew when a person around her was sinful. She could "smell" him or her and become physically ill. She died on June 1, 1902, was beatified by Pius XI in 1933, and was canonized on May 2, 1940, by Pius XII.

The Blessed Virgin Mary Appeared to Them

Our Lady in Lourdes

FOURTEEN-YEAR-OLD *Bernadette Soubirous* was with her younger sister and a companion picking up firewood near a natural grotto in the vicinity of Lourdes when she heard the rustling sound of the wind. Suddenly, she saw a bright light surrounding a smiling woman dressed in white with a light-blue sash appearing to stand on a rose tree in the grotto. Bernadette took out her rosary and began praying as the woman, running her fingers on her beads, joined her. Telling her to come back every day for fifteen days, the woman said, "I don't promise to make you happy in this world but in the next. Pray for sinners." Then, she exhorted her to spread a message to the world, saying, "Penance! Penance!" The news of the apparition began to spread. The following day, Mary appeared again and told Bernadette to drink from a spring she pointed to a spot on the ground. As the Saint dug into the ground, she appeared to spectators to be eating mud. Then, the Lady said to Bernadette, "Tell the priests to build a chapel here." The apparition took place eighteen times as curious crowds began to swell. On the last apparition, Mary revealed herself as the Immaculate Conception. Four years earlier, in 1854, Pope

Pius IX had proclaimed the Immaculate Conception of Mary as dogma of faith (*HF/ES*).

Bernadette suffered a lot of opposition from her family, her neighbors, the clergy, and even civil authorities who put her in prison. (This writer, his wife, son Mark, stepdaughter Christine, and eight other pilgrims were fortunate to have attended a mass by a Polish chaplain in that prison room twenty-six years ago.) The bishop appointed a commission to investigate the apparition. After three years, the findings supported St. Bernadette's claims. Meanwhile, Lourdes became a destination for pilgrims and tourists. Lourdes' water was found to have healing powers, not by its natural characteristics but through Mary's intercession. A beautiful chapel was built near the spring upon the urging of Empress Eugenie, wife of Napoleon III.

Two years after the apparitions, Bernadette attended school free of tuition with the Sisters of Charity. Later in 1866, she went to live with the Sisters of Notre Dame in Nevers, where she experienced harsh treatment from the mistress of novices. She worked hard as an infirmarian and sacristan; she suffered from tuberculosis of the bone in her right knee. When told to go to Lourdes for a cure, she replied, "The place is for others, not for me. It's my duty to bear my illness." She died on September 22, 1879. She was beatified in 1925 by Pius XI and canonized by him in 1933. Lourdes became a pilgrims' destination and tourist place where many miracles were attributed to Mary's intercession.

Our Lady in Fátima

(Source: *The True Story of Fátima: A Complete Account of the Fátima Apparitions* by John de Marchi, IMC)

Three little shepherd cousins—*Lucia,* 10; *Francisco,* 9; and *Jacinta,* 7—were in a cave and playing jacks after praying the rosary when an angel appeared to them, saying, "Fear not! I am the Angel of Peace. Pray with me." With them, he prayed the prayer he taught them: "My God, I believe, I adore, I hope, and I love

Thee." They also asked God's pardon for those who didn't believe in God. Before disappearing, he told them to repeat the prayer as often as they could to repair the sins of ingratitude to the heart of Jesus. Months later, the angel appeared again, this time revealing himself as the guardian angel of Portugal. He asked them to make sacrifices to God for the conversion of their country. In the third and last apparition, the angel held a chalice and a host that dripped blood into it. After prostrating on the ground, leaving the chalice and host over it suspended in midair, he prayed to the Holy Trinity and offered Christ in the tabernacles of the world in reparation for all the sacrileges and offenses against His Sacred Heart. Arising and saying "Take and drink the Body and Blood of Jesus, horribly outraged by ungrateful men. Make reparation for their crimes against God," he gave the host to Lucia and the content of the chalice to Francisco and Jacinta. The children's experience with the angel left in them a lingering, happy feeling of the presence of God.

Lucia was the youngest of seven children of Jesus, a farmer, and Maria Rosa dos Santos. The couple owned lands scattered in the hamlet of Aljustrel, part of the village of Fátima. Francisco and Jacinta were the eighth and ninth children of Ti and Olimpia Matos, sister of Lucia's father. Every morning, the three children would come together to let their sheep out of the barn, take them to pasture in neighboring hamlets, eat lunch at the stroke of the church noon bells, recite the rosary, play jacks, and then lead the sheep back to the fold at the sound of the Angelus bells.

The First Apparition: On Sunday, May 13, 1917, the children were playing building, gathering rocks to build a "castle" in Cova da Iria, a stony area full of brushes near Fátima, when they suddenly saw a bright light they took as warning for an approaching rain. Although the sun above them was bright and the sky was cloudless, they gathered the sheep and started down the hill. Halfway down past a tall oak tree, they became afraid when another flash of light hit the sky, prompting them to turn in front of a small holm oak. Suddenly, they saw a beautiful lady dressed in white—more brilliant than the sun—standing on top of the oak's foliage. The Lady said,

NICHOLAS LLANES ROSAL, STD, PHL, MSJ

"Fear not. I'll not harm you." Lucia asked, "Where are you from?" "I'm from heaven," the Lady said. She asked them to return there at the same hour every thirteenth day for six consecutive months, promising them, "I'll tell you later who I am and what I want." Her innocence exuding, Lucia asked her, "And I . . . am I going to go to heaven?" The Lady assured her she would but also Jacinta and Francisco if the young boy would "say many rosaries."

Then the Lady asked, *"Do you want to offer yourselves to God to endure all the sufferings that He may choose to send you, as an act of reparation for the sins by which He is offended and as a plea for the conversion of sinners?"* Lucia answered for all three, *"Yes, we want to."* *"Then you are going to suffer a great deal,"* the Lady said, *"but the grace of God will be your comfort."* Instinctively, the children uttered the prayer taught by the angel. The Lady said, *"Pray the Rosary every day to bring peace to the world and the end of the war."* World War I then was in progress. Before disappearing into the sky, the Lady opened her hands and radiated an intense light into the children that made them see themselves in God as in a mirror.

The children were ecstatic the rest of the day. But Francisco who saw the Lady but was kept out of the conversation pressed the two to tell him what the Lady had said. When told that the Lady promised he would go to heaven, he jumped with joy, saying, "Oh, my Lady, I will say all the rosaries you want!" All three promised to keep everything a secret. However, when Jacinta arrived home, the first thing she wanted to do was tell her mother about it. Olimpia wasn't home when Jacinta arrived, but when Jacinta saw her in front of the house, coming home from the market, she ran to meet her to tell her about the visitor from heaven. Olimpia couldn't believe a little girl like her daughter could have seen Our Lady. But because Francisco too had seen her, their father was starting to believe. The following morning, Olimpia repeated to her neighbors her children's story. The word spread, and Olimpia's sister-in-law, Lucia's mother, heard about it. She and her entire household became angry. They accused Lucia of lying. Even their neighbors ridiculed the young girl. Then, Lucia remembered what the Lady had told her and her cousins: "You are going to suffer a great deal."

The Second Apparition: Lucia's mother went to consult with the pastor, who suggested to let her return to the Cova da Iria the following thirteenth (a big parish feast day of St. Anthony) although he wanted to see them after that day. The day arrived for the second apparition. A crowd decided to go to the Cova instead of going to the parish feast. The Lady came. Lucia asked her to cure a sick person for whom she was asked to intercede. Our Lady told her, "If he is converted, he will be cured within a year." Then she said, *"I will take Jacinta and Francisco soon. You, however, are to stay here a longer time. Jesus wants to use you to make me known and loved. He wants to establish the Devotion to my Immaculate Heart in the world. I promise salvation to those who embrace it."* Our Lady then told Lucia her wish—in between the mysteries of the rosary, the following prayer should be said: *"O my Jesus, forgive us our sins, save us from the fires of help, lead all souls to Heaven, especially those most in need."* The people saw Lucia speaking to someone but could only hear a voice like a "gentle humming of bee."

After this apparition, the pastor met with the three children in the rectory, expecting to hear a unique message from Our Lady. He was greatly disappointed. The children revealed nothing, causing him to say the apparitions were a hoax, a devil's trick. Struggling with the pastor's conclusion, Lucia began to doubt the reality of Our Lady's apparitions and was tempted to announce to everyone that everything was a lie. Her innocent little cousins told her, "If you say that, you'd be lying and lying is a sin." That night, Lucia dreamed of the devil dragging her to hell and laughing at her because he had succeeded in deceiving her. Waking up, she called Our Lady so loud that she awakened her mother.

The Third Apparition: The morning of July 13 came. Suddenly, all doubt disappeared from Lucia. Walking over to her cousins' home, she found them kneeling, praying, and crying. Seeing their cousin, they jumped up and walked joyfully with her to the Cova. Being with Our Lady once again, Lucia asked, "What do you want of me?" The Lady repeated her request to pray the rosary every day for the conversion of sinners and for the end of the war, for

NICHOLAS LLANES ROSAL, STD, PHL, MSJ

"only Our Lady of the Rosary can end the war." Again, Our Lady reminded her to sacrifice themselves in reparation for sins committed against her Immaculate Heart and Jesus' heart. "She opened her hands again . . . The light reflecting from them seemed to penetrate into the earth, and we saw as if (the light penetrated) into a sea of fire, and immersed in that fire were devils and souls in human form . . . floating in the fire and swayed by the flames . . . amidst wailing and cries of pain and despair . . . (It) horrified and shook us with terror," Lucia would later write about the terrifying vision.

Our Lady then said, *"You have seen hell—where the souls of sinners go. To save them, God wants to establish throughout the world the devotion to my Immaculate Heart . . . If (sinners) do not stop offending God, another and worse war will break out in the reign of Pius XI. When you see a night illumined by an unknown light, know that it is the great sign that God gives you that He is going to punish the world for its crimes by means of war, hunger, persecution of the Church and of the Holy Father."* She also asked that the Holy Father consecrate Russia to her Immaculate Heart and that the Communion of Reparation on the first Saturdays be observed.

In response, the children made many sacrifices. When thirsty, they denied themselves drink. When hungry, they fasted more, giving their food to hungry children in the neighborhood. When sick, they offered the pain and their sleeplessness. When ridiculed, they bore it. Tired, they continued to pray and tend the sheep. Feeling wanting to play or dance to the music of Francisco's flute, they would mortify themselves. They vied with one another to find ways to sacrifice more. They amazed their parents with the sacrifices they made—all to obey Our Lady's wishes: for the conversion of sinners; for the safety of the Holy Father; for the greater honor of God the Father, the Son, and the Holy Spirit; for the war to end; for the healing of the sick; for people to love the Blessed Sacrament more; for priests and nuns . . .

The fourth apparition didn't happen on the thirteenth. That day, the magistrate, a Freemason, kidnapped them, threatened them with burning oil, and when he could get no secrets from them, he put them in prison to prevent them from going to the Cova. They spent that night very scared to be with older prisoners. The following day, afraid of raging demonstrations by the people for kidnapping the children, the magistrate himself took the children in his carriage to Fátima. Our Lady liberated them. She saw them on the nineteenth.

At about four o'clock, Lucia with her cousins happened to be in Valinhos, in the vicinity of the Cova, when a radiant light coming from the east announced the appearance of the Lady. She stood on a holm oak, which was slightly taller than the one at the Cova. Intently looking at the radiant face of the heavenly visitor, the three children listened to her as she told them, *"I want you to continue to come to the Cova de Iria on the thirteenth and to continue to say the rosary every day."* Knowing that the past July-thirteenth apparition did not take place, the children took the message as even more comforting and encouraging. They felt the Lady did not abandon them like many in the community who didn't believe them. Lucia told Our Lady of her anguish at the unbelief of the apparitions and asked her if she would perform a miracle so that all might see and believe. "Yes," Our Lady replied. *"In the last month, in October, I shall perform a miracle so that all may believe in my apparitions. If they had not taken you to the village, the miracle would be greater. Saint Joseph will come with the Baby Jesus to give peace to the world. The Lord will come to bless the people. Besides, Our Lady of the Rosary and Our Lady of Sorrows will come."* Our Lady also instructed Lucia who complained of accusations that the apparitions were only a money-making gimmick. Our Lady advised that the donations that had started to come in be used for litters on the Feast of Our Lady of the Rosary and for the construction of a chapel. Before leaving, Our Lady again reminded the children to pray a great deal and make sacrifices for sinners and for many who go to hell because no one prays and makes sacrifices for them.

The Fifth Apparition: As the children walked from home to the Cova, people lined up the streets: the lame, the sick, and the people asking the children to intercede for them. Some people remarked the scene reminded them of the people who lined up

NICHOLAS LLANES ROSAL, STD, PHL, MSJ

along the streets of Judea to see Jesus, hoping to be cured. Before the apparition, people witnessed a globe coming from the east and coming down to settle on the holm oak where she always stood. Our Lady said to Lucia, "In October, I shall perform a miracle so that all may believe in my apparitions. Had they not taken you to the village, the miracle would be greater. St. Joseph and the Baby Jesus will come to give peace to the world. Our Lady of the Rosary and Our Lady of Sorrows will come." Then she promised to cure within a year some of the sick for whom Lucia interceded. But again, she insisted on the need for the world to pray, to make sacrifices for sinners, "for many will go to hell for not having someone to pray and make sacrifices for them."

Several priests were among the crowd at that apparition. One of them, a monsignor, wrote, "Father Gois chose a spot overlooking the vast amphitheater of the Cova. At noontime, silence fell on the crowd, and a low whispering of prayers could be heard. Suddenly, cries of joy rent the air, many voices praising the Blessed Virgin. Arms were raised to point to something above. 'Look! Don't you see? . . . Yes, I see it . . . a luminous globe, coming from the east to the west, gliding slowly and majestically through space . . .'" Other signs were reported that day. People could see the stars even though it was midday. There was a rain of iridescent petals that vanished upon reaching the ground. People left amazed, hopefully not forgetting the mother of God's message of prayer and sacrifice.

Examples of how the children made sacrifices were many. Jacinta's mother brought her and her companions grapes (which she loved a lot) one day, and they were about to eat them when Jacinta said, "Let's not eat them but give them to the children there," pointing to children on the street several feet away. On another occasion, a lady friend of their families gave them figs to eat. Although hungry, they kept them until they could give them away to other children. Closely watching their sheep one day, Lucia found a rope on the ground, and Francisco suggested that it be cut into three pieces so that everyone could wear it on the skin around the waist to atone for the sins of unbelievers. The Lady, however, told the children to remove them while in bed.

The Sixth Apparition: People had come from near and far to Iria where Mary, Our Lady, was reported to appear at one o'clock in the afternoon of October 13, 1917. Thousands had traveled for days to reach the Cova da Iria. Some of the rich came in sleek automobiles, the pilgrims and sightseers in carriages, and the poor in their carts or on the backs of donkeys while many more walked miles and miles on muddy roads, for rain had started the night before, even as rain continued into the morning until noon. Newspapers, like Lisbon's *O Século*, reported that when the crowds were about settled in anticipation of the event, there must have been between seventy thousand and one hundred thousand people, including priests and nuns, believers and unbelievers, groups singing religious hymns, and a few others who, induced by Freemasons and other anti-Catholic critics, heckled and hurled antichurch epithets.

Senhora da Capelinha, a family friend of the Matoses and dos Santoses, wrote about a priest who had spent the night at the Cova reading his breviary. She wrote, "When the children arrived, dressed as if for first communion, he asked them about the time of the apparition. 'At noon.' Lucia responded. The priest took out his watch and said, 'Look, it is already noon.' 'Our Lady never lies. Let us wait.' A few minutes went by. He looked at his watch again. 'Noon is gone. Everyone out of here! The whole thing is an illusion!' Lucia did not want to leave, so the priest began pushing the three children away. Lucia, almost in tears, said, 'Whoever wants may go away. I'm not going. I'm on my own property. Our Lady said she was coming. She always came before and so she must be coming again.' Just then, she glanced towards the east and said to Jacinta, 'Jacinta, kneel down. Our Lady is coming. I've seen the flash.' The priest was silenced. I never saw him again."

"Silence. Silence! Our Lady is coming!" Lucia cried out. She came. John de Marchi, IMC, writes, "Her snow-white feet rested on the beautiful flowers and ribbons with which Senora da Capelinha had adorned the tree. The faces of the three children assumed an unworldly expression, their features becoming more delicate, their color mellow, their eyes intent upon the Lady.

"'What do you want of me?'

"'I want a chapel to be built in my honor. _I am Our Lady of the Rosary_. Continue to say the Rosary every day. The war will end soon, and the soldiers will return to their homes.'

"'Do you want anything more?'

"'Nothing more.'

"As Our Lady took leave, she opened her hands which emitted a flood of light. While she was rising, she pointed toward the sun and the light gleaming from her hands brightened the sun itself.

"'There she goes, there she goes!' Lucia shouted. The multitude roared, echoing her cry in wonder as the clouds parted then disappeared, revealing a pale sun."

To the left of the sun appeared St. Joseph holding the child Jesus, blessing the world three times with the sign of the cross. Our Lady, in her blue-and-white robe as the Queen of the Most Holy Rosary, stood on the right of the sun. As Lucia, Jacinta, and Francisco gazed at the sun, they saw Jesus dressed in a red robe as the Redeemer, and beside Him was Our Lady clothed now in purple as Our Lady of Sorrows and then changed to a simple brown robe as Our Lady of Mt. Carmel. The thousands were witnessing a phenomenon never seen before.

The Portuguese newspaper _O Dia_ describes the vision in the following manner: "The sky had a certain greyish tint of pearl and a strange clearness filled the gloomy landscape, every moment getting gloomier. The sun seemed veiled with transparent gauze to enable us to look at it without difficulty. The greyish tint of mother-of-pearl began changing as if into a shining silver disc, that was growing slowly until it broke through the clouds. And the silver sun, still shrouded in the same greyish lightness of gauze, was seen to rotate and wander within the circle of the receded clouds! The people cried out with one voice, the thousands of the creatures of God whom faith raised up to Heaven fell to their knees upon the muddy ground."

O Século, a Lisbon newspaper, reported, "Suddenly, the people broke out with a cry of extreme anguish. **The sun, still rotating, had unloosened itself from the skies and came hurtling towards**

the earth. This huge, fiery millstone threatened to crush us with its weight. It was a dreadful sensation."

All were kneeling in the mud, waiting for the end of the world. There was a "godless man" who had been making fun of "the simpletons" at Iria just to see a girl. Father Lourenco, who was present at the site, said, "I looked at him and he was numbed, his eyes riveted on the sun. I saw him tremble from head to foot. Then he raised his hands towards heaven as he was kneeling there in the mud and cried out, 'Our Lady, Our Lady.' Everyone was crying and weeping, asking God to forgive them their sins. When this was over, we ran to the chapels, some to one, others to the other in our village . . . When everyone realized the danger was over, there was an outburst of joy. Everyone broke out in a hymn of praise to Our Lady."

After the miracle, the three children appeared to be back to their routine, but they knew what the future awaited them: Francisco and Jacinta would soon go to heaven while Lucia would stay to spread the devotion to the Immaculate Heart of Mary. Meanwhile, people would never miss the opportunity to talk to them, asking them the same questions asked them a thousand times before. But they remained faithful to Our Lady, keeping the secret entrusted to them, praying, and sacrificing for the conversion of sinners and the safety of the Holy Father.

Francisco was asked many times what he would like to be when he grew up. Nothing, not even to be a priest. "I don't want to do anything. I just want to die and go to heaven" was his reply. The rest of his life may be summed up in his own words when asked about the apparitions: "What I liked best about the apparitions was seeing Our Lord in that light that the Blessed Virgin put into our hearts. I love God very much. He is so sad because of so many sins. *We must not commit even the smallest sin.*" An influenza epidemic struck the area, confining Francisco and Jacinta in bed. Both would take all the medicine—however bitter—gladly without any complaint as penance "to make Our Lady and Jesus happy." Both would never cease praying. Their mother said, "They pray the rosary at least seven or eight times every day, and there was no end to their short prayers." Francisco asked to make his confession and receive communion. Before the priest came, he asked Jacinta and Lucia what sins they could remember so that he could confess them. Jacinta reminded him of the ten pennies he stole. But Francisco said he already confessed that. The priest came to hear his confession. The following morning when he heard the tinkling bell to announce the arrival of the priest, he tried to sit up but could not. After he received the Body of Jesus, he asked his mother if the priest would come back the following morning again to give him communion, but that wouldn't happen. He would go to heaven early the following morning of April 4, 1919. Jacinta was so sick she couldn't attend the funeral.

Jacinta's condition became worse every day. An abscess had developed on her chest. A visiting doctor suggested that she be brought to the hospital in Ourém, many miles away from home. She knew that no medical treatment would keep her alive, but she went along because of the opportunity to sacrifice more for the Blessed Virgin. Separating from her family and Lucia was a painful suffering to bear on top of the physical agony of being transported by her father on a donkey's back to a distant hospital. The doctors gave her the best they could offer, but their efforts were futile. After two months, they decided to send her home. Our Lady comforted her at home but told her to go to Lisbon for treatment. Lisbon was even farther away, and she was now sadly thinking she was going to die alone. But on the advice of a doctor and a priest, she and her mother journeyed to Lisbon. Arriving there, nobody could take them in except the Orphanage of Our Lady of the Miracles. The mother superior, a kindly woman, gave every attention to them, especially to the sick Jacinta. Jacinta liked the place because there was a chapel where she could stay for as long as she wanted to commune with Jesus in the Blessed Sacrament. There were twenty-five children with whom she could talk and play. The superior said later that Our Lady visited her more than once.

Jacinta and the mother superior conversed a lot that revealed the nine-year-old's spiritual maturity. They talked about confession, mortification, chastity, the Blessed Sacrament, and even government. Then, the doctors came and took her to surgery. She suffered a lot. The anesthesia did not help much. The procedure opened a wound the size of a fist, but she bore the pain with patience, even telling Our Lady, "Patience, patience, Our Lady! We must suffer to go to heaven." Then, talking to Jesus, she said, "Now you can convert many sinners, for I suffer a great deal, my Jesus." Sounds like Santa Teresa de Jesus bantering with Jesus. Yet she was only nine years old! Four days after the operation, she asked for a priest to hear her confession and to give her the last anointing and communion. The priest came, heard her confession, anointed her, but decided to give her communion the next morning. At ten thirty that evening, February 20, 1920, away from home, she died, with Aurora Gomez, the nurse, by her side. *Francisco* and *Jacinta* were beatified by Pope John Paul in Fátima, Portugal, on May 13, 2000.

Three months after the last apparition, Rome appointed Joseph Correia da Silva as bishop of a new diocese that had jurisdiction over Fátima. The bishop started slowly and carefully to investigate the reality and meaning of the miracles. He called *Lucia dos Santos* and her mother to tell them of his decision to protect Lucia's privacy and to secure her as the primary trustworthy witness of the miracles. To protect her privacy, Lucia was given a new name (Maria das Dores) and instructed to go live in a convent where no one knew her. With the sisters of St. Dorothy, Lucia continued with her prayers and penance as the Blessed Virgin continued to appear to her. On December 10, 1925, she showed her bleeding heart surrounded by thorns. Our Lady urged Lucia to spread the First Saturday Devotion, telling her to work through the mother superior.

In 1929, the Blessed Mother appeared to her again, warning her that war would come soon—worse than the one just passed—if people didn't repent. At this apparition, the Blessed Mother also put up a sign—an unexplainable appearance of the northern lights—that should prompt the world to repent. In particular, Our Lady asked that the Holy Father consecrate Russia to her Immaculate Heart. Of serious concern was the spread of atheistic Communism that had engulfed European countries occupied by Russia and was now encroaching upon parts of Asia. On October 31, 1942, Pius XII consecrated the world to the Immaculate Heart of Mary, but Russia was only obliquely mentioned.

In 1948, Sister Lucy became a Carmelite nun and again wrote letters to the bishop of Leiria and the Vatican, urging the Holy Father and all the bishops of the world to consecrate Russia. She insisted that the consecration of Russia was key to world peace. On the occasion of the beatification of Francisco and Jacinta, Pope John Paul consecrated the world again to the Immaculate Heart of Mary, but like in the previous consecration by Pius XII, Russia was not mentioned. Sister Lucia continued to pray and do penance for the world, but she died on February 13, 2005, at the age of ninety-seven. On the third anniversary of her death, Pope Benedict XVI announced her canonization process to be put on the fast track, the same process that would speed up Pope John Paul's and Mother Teresa's canonizations. Sister Lucia's body was laid to rest alongside the bodies of her cousins Francisco and Jacinta at the Fátima Shrine in Coimbra, Portugal. *Holy Fátima Children, pray for us!*

As *St. Dominic* knelt in the chapel of Notre Dame in Prouille, Our Lady appeared to him with a rosary. Instructing him on how to pray it, she assured him that the rosary would be his support in converting heretics and the weapon of Christian nations against their enemies. St. Dominic went out preaching the devotion as he met with heretics. Through the intercession of the Blessed Mother, St. Dominic was said to have converted more than one hundred thousand heretics and sinners. At the Battle of Muret in 1213, the Christian army, taught by St. Dominic to pray the rosary, attributed their victory over the Albigensian soldiers not only with their weapons of war but also by the power of the Lady of the Most Holy Rosary.

On October 7, 1571, Don Juan of Austria battled the Turkish fleet at Lepanto, relying on the help of Our Lady of the Rosary. Reflecting that reliance, his soldiers cried out "Ave Maria" at every volley they shot into the enemy ships at the same time that confraternities of the holy rosary walked in procession on the streets of Rome, devoutly praying the rosary. Don Juan's victory saved

Europe from becoming Islamic. The Venetian Senate declared, "It was not the generals nor battalions nor arms that brought us victory, but it was Our Lady of the Rosary." In thanksgiving, Pius V ordered October 7 as a day to commemorate Our Lady of Victory. In 1574, Gregory XIII decreed that day as the Feast of our Lady of the Rosary. Many other popes—including Leo XIII, Pius XII, and Pope John Paul—urged the world to pray the rosary for peace and conversion of sinners. The miracles in Lourdes and Fátima confirmed the need of Christians and the rest of the world to rely on the Blessed Mother's power to save everyone from physical and spiritual ruin and to spare the world from Communism and self-destruction (*HF/ES*).

St. Bernard of Clairvaux, a Cistercian abbot and doctor of the church, as a child dreamed of Mary and the baby Jesus. Among the works he was known for was his being called as judge to arbitrate the claims of Innocent II and Amaeletus II to the papacy. A mystic, he wrote several treatises on the union of the soul with God here and in the next life as the purpose of man's existence. He also preached the Second Crusade and countered the theological errors of Abelard and of Gilbert, bishop of Poitiers. His devotion to the Blessed Virgin made him write numerous sermons about her. Persistently bothered by poor health, he became very ill one day and went to pray at the altars of Mary and Sts. Lawrence and Benedict. The Saints and Mary appeared to him and placed their hands on his abdomen, healing him instantly.

In his anger toward St. John Damascene, who was known for defending the veneration of statues during the iconoclast era in the East, Emperor Leo III forged a letter with the Saint's signature and sent it to the caliph in Damascus. The letter, falsely relating the Saint's intent to betray the city to the caliph's enemies, angered the caliph, who ordered John's hand to be cut off. St. John prayed to the Blessed Virgin. He fell asleep by her image, and when he awoke, his hand had been restored.

(Reflection: The Blessed Mother's miracles in Fátima reveal to us the intimate relationship of the church's doctrine of Mary's divine motherhood and the doctrine of Christ, her Son, as our Redeemer. When we honor Mary, we honor her Son. When we glorify Christ, we glorify Mary. When we offend her, we offend her Son. In all her apparitions to the children, the Blessed Mother made that intimate connection between herself and Jesus very clear. For that reason, Mary continually asked the children to pray and make sacrifices for the sins that saddened her and her Son. From the beginning, Our Lady asked them, *"Do you want to offer yourselves to God, to endure all the sufferings that He may choose to send you, as an act of reparation for the sins by which He is offended and as a plea for the conversion of sinners?"* Lucia answered yes for the three, and all three spent their lives suffering for the reparation of sins and conversion of sinners. Jacinta's statement to Jesus after a painful operation days before her death sums up how true they were to their word to Our Lady: *"Now you can convert many sinners, for I suffer a great deal, my Jesus."* Where can you find such simplicity, such innocence, and such purity but in the soul of this nine-year-old!)

Through the miracles, Mary confirmed the existence of purgatory, where Lucia's friend still remained. She revealed hell—the place of the damned—where many bad people go because, according to Our Lady, there are not enough people to pray for sinners to convert. To help, Mary asked that the special prayer—"Jesus, forgive us our sins, save us from the fires of hell . . ."—be inserted in between the mysteries. Little Jacinta had an idea as to how to avoid hell. "Confession is a sacrament of mercy," she said, speaking like a preacher. "That is why people should approach the confessional with confidence and joy. *Without confession, there is no salvation.*" From the mouth of babes!

Still living on earth, the children, because of their closeness to Mary, became intercessors. People placed their hopes for their loved ones to be cured by asking the children to remember them to Our Lady. Jacinta remarked, "They trust us because we see Our Lady. How much more trust will they have if they themselves see Jesus!"

In every apparition, Our Lady stressed the importance of praying the rosary every day. She identified herself as the Queen of the Rosary. Through her, people can hope for eternal salvation by meditating on the mysteries and following what they teach. Faithfully following them makes one a true follower of Christ. The rosary is a powerful instrument Mary has handed to the world to assure us of bonding with Jesus. Francisco was convinced that through the rosary, he would go to heaven. "I'll pray as many rosaries as Our Lady wants as long as I go to heaven," he said. So should we say and do! As the Latin saying affirms, *"Ad Jesum per Mariam!"* (To Jesus through Mary).

The miracle on October 13, 1917, confirmed and strengthened the faith of believers in Our Lady, led many to convert, and put the enemies of the faith to shame. Today, the miracle continues to strengthen the faith of people devoted to Mary and serves to draw more people to her. In Lourdes and Fátima, not to mention Medjugorje and every Marian shrine in the world, countless pilgrims go to Mary to fulfill her wishes for peace and conversion of sinners. Through worldwide prayers for the conversion of Russia, it's heartening to know that Christianity is now allowed and practiced there although much more has to be done. Many other countries, including the United States, that are making laws that hurt religious freedom or hinder people from practicing their Christian faith call for a lot of prayers and sacrifices.

An important part of the story of Fátima is the role of the angel of Portugal, who prepared the children for the apparitions of the Blessed Virgin. The angel taught them how to pray to the Almighty and made them aware of the need to pray for sinners—a persistent message Our Lady later told them to do. Angels have been part of the life of Mary, starting at the annunciation, through the birth of Jesus, Christ's crucifixion and resurrection, at her assumption to heaven, and finally, at her coronation as Queen of Heaven and her proclamation by Christians as Queen of the Angels. As in the miracles of Jesus where God used angels as His instruments, angels are presumed to assist Mary in the miracles that have been attributed to her loving intercession over the centuries. In our recitation of the rosary, angels are part of the mysteries we meditate on—the first joyful mystery (the annunciation), the third (the nativity), the fourth and fifth sorrowful mysteries, the first glorious mystery (the resurrection), the third, and especially the fourth (the assumption) and fifth glorious mysteries (the coronation of the Blessed Virgin).

Our Lady, Queen of the Angels

Angels see the face of the Father, Jesus said (Mt 18:10), ever ready to do what the Father tells them to do. Surrounding His throne, they are the hosts of heaven (Jb 1:6, 2:1), the armed forces of God (Gn 32:21). In the Old Testament days, they were the ministers of God's law, helping and blessing those, like Abraham and Sarah, who obeyed it but punishing others, like those in Sodom and Gomorrah, who disobeyed. God created them in hierarchical order, according to St. Paul (Eph 1:21) and St. Thomas Aquinas. He organized them by choir, starting with the choir of angels, then of the archangels, principalities, dominations, virtues, powers, thrones, cherubim, and seraphim. They are all God's messengers and instruments of His divine providence to help and guide mankind to heaven.

The Bible names three of them: *St. Michael,* the leading angel (Jude 9), who, with his angels, won over the dragon (Apoc. 12) and will arouse the dead on Judgment Day (1 Thes 4:16). *St. Raphael,* whose name means "God has healed" (Tb 12:15), one of seven in the presence of the Lord (Tb 3:16) who was commanded to come down in the form of man, taking the name Azaria, to bring sight to Tobias and conduct Tobit, his son, to Raguel, whom Tobit took to be his holy bride. And *St. Gabriel,* whose name means "God is powerful," who interceded for mankind at the deluge, explained to Daniel the meaning of the ram and goat and the "70 years" (Dn 9:21-27), announced to incredulous Zachary the birth of his son, John the Baptist (Lk 1:11-20), and finally appeared to Mary to persuade her to become the mother of the Most High as eternally planned by God the Father for mankind's salvation (Lk 1:26-38).

Serving as messengers and guardians, they announced the birth of the Messiah (Lk 2:8-13) then warned the three kings to return to their countries by another route to protect the Child King from being killed by Herod. They told St. Joseph to leave Judea with Mary and baby Jesus to escape the massacre of innocents (Mt 2:13). (*Let's pray: "Oh, merciful Father, increase the host of angels on earth to protect the innocent infants from being massacred every day. This we ask* through *the intercession of your Blessed Mother. Amen."*) They ministered to Jesus at the desert after He confounded Satan (Mt 4:4), comforted Him at the garden of Gethsemane, and then announced His resurrection to the women and the apostles (Mt 28:2). They guided the apostles, comforted the martyrs, and stood by the Saints through the centuries unto our times to keep watch over us. Then, they will come to pick up the dust of the dead and, with God's power, join their souls into the bodies and take them resurrected before the throne of Christ the King on the final Judgment Day. In triumph, they will accompany the blessed into the gates of heaven forever and ever to celebrate with them their final victory over sin and death.

Angels primarily look after the spiritual good of people although they are committed to protect the physical welfare of humans for the good of their souls. They continually look after us all as they have taken care of the Saints.

At age eighteen, *Thomas Aquinas* entered the Dominican Order. Opposed to Thomas' decision, his family detained him in the tower of the family castle for two years. To make him lose interest in religious life, his two younger brothers introduced a woman of ill repute into his room. As soon as Thomas saw the woman, he picked up a burning brand from the hearth and drove her away then traced a cross on the wall. Kneeling before the cross, he asked God to give him the gift of perpetual chastity. He fell into an ecstasy wherein two angels appeared and girded him with a cord that would remind him for the rest of his life the God-given gift of chastity. He died at age fifty after living a brilliant, intellectual, and spiritually uplifting life by the side of his angel. St. Thomas is known as the Angelic Doctor, among other reasons, for his intellectual acumen and singular faith that enabled him to explain about God almost in a manner by which angels see Him (i.e., in His divine essence as the

Good) (1 *Summa* Q 62, art 8 c). After that miraculous event, to this day, members of the Dominican Order, including tertiaries, wear the girdle around their bodies as a special spiritual devotion and penitential practice *(ES)*.

St. Frances of Rome, founder of the Oblates of Mary in the fourteenth century, was said to have had two angels at birth, but no angel appeared to her until her son, Evangelista, died. At early dawn of her son's first death anniversary, her oratory suddenly shone with a brilliant light as she saw her son with an archangel. Evangelista told her that God was giving her the archangel, who looked like a handsome nine-year-old boy, to look after her in her old age. Receiving him, Frances fell to her knees, asking him to help her against the devil who persistently tempted her. The archangel followed her wherever she went, surrounding her with a halo that only she could see. At night, she did not need a candle; her angel's radiance supplied the light. The archangel stayed with her for twenty-four years until another angel, a power, succeeded him. In his human form, he was even more beautiful than the archangel. The power's mere presence prevented the evil one from approaching Frances up close. He carried three golden palm branches symbolizing the three virtues Frances wanted to develop in her soul: charity, prudence, and patience. Frances was known to have multiplied food for the sick, the needy, and the prisoners. Her sister's withered hand was restored as she washed the Saint's body for burial. St. Frances was canonized in 1608 by Pope Paul V *(ES)*.

Angels intimately interacted with the Saints in accordance with the words of the psalmist: God has charged the angels "over us to keep us in our ways." *St. Cecilia's* angel was always around her, becoming visible to her husband, *Valerian,* and his brother, *Tiburtius,* after they were baptized *(HF)*. *St. Agnes* was protected from the soldiers who threatened her with their swords. *St. Germaine's* angel parted the waters of the stream to enable her to go to church and attend mass. *St. Isidore's* angel plowed with him to double the fruits of his labor so that he could share more with the poor and the church *(ES)*. *St. Zita's* angel baked bread and cleaned the house for her so that she could stay longer in church, praying and talking to Jesus in the Blessed Sacrament (*ES*). *Padre Pio* had an angel who acted as his ambassador to deal with angels of other people who needed help from him. "If you need my help," Padre Pio said, "talk to your guardian angels to talk to my own angel" (*ES*). And the list goes on and on of angels' work with humans whom they want to bring to heaven. No less than a seraph brought crucified Jesus down to St. Francis, and the Saint received stigmatic wounds (*ES*). Before the apparitions of the Blessed Virgin to the *three children* in Fátima, the angel of Portugal appeared to them, teaching them a special prayer to the Holy Trinity for their country and for sinners. The angelic apparitions prepared them to meet Our Lady (*HF*).

CONCLUSION

Miracle Recipients: Why Them?

*B*ECAUSE THEY HAVE *faith*—an unwavering faith—*and love.* Jesus Himself said, *"Have faith in God.* Amen I say to you, whoever says to the mountain, 'Arise and hurl yourself into the sea,' and does not waiver in his heart, but believes that whatever he says will be done, it shall be done for him" (Mk 11:23-24). They have faith rooted in love as St. Paul says, "And if I have prophecy and know all the mysteries and all knowledge, and if I have all faith so as to remove mountains, **yet do not have love,** <u>*I am nothing*</u>" (1 Cor 13:2-3). A sincere faith is rooted in love of God and neighbor.

Because they ask for it. "And when he had come to the crowd, a man approached him and threw himself on his knees before him, saying, *'Lord, have pity on my son,* for he is a lunatic and suffers severely . . .' (And Jesus said,) 'Bring him here to me' and Jesus rebuked him, and the devil went out of him, and from that moment, the boy was cured" (Mk 17:14-17). And as Jesus was approaching Jericho, a blind man by the wayside repeatedly cried out, *"Jesus, Son of David, have mercy on me!"* When Jesus saw him, He asked, "What wouldst thou have me do for thee?" And the blind man said, *"Lord, that I may see."* And Jesus said, "Receive thy sight. Thy faith has saved thee" (Lk 18:37-42). Effective prayer is sincere, earnest, and persevering. "For everyone who asks, receives, and he who seeks finds" (Mt 7:8-9).

Because their sins have been forgiven. "And behold, some men were carrying upon a pallet a man who was paralyzed and they were trying to bring him in and to lay him before him. And as they found no way of bringing him in because of the crowd, they went up onto the roof, and lowered him through the tiles with his pallet into the midst before Jesus. And seeing their faith, he said, 'Man, *thy sins are forgiven thee.'* . . . He said to the paralytic, "Arise, take up thy pallet and go to thy home" (Mk 5:18-24). We note that other miracles Jesus performed were preceded by His forgiving their sins, putting sinners in the state of grace. A clean heart makes prayer effective and pleasing to God.

Because they are resigned to the will of God and God wills it. There was a man who besought Jesus, saying, *"Lord, if thou wilt,* thou canst make me clean." Stretching forth His arm, Jesus touched him, saying, **"I will.** Be thou made clean." And immediately the leprosy left him (Lk 5:12-14). We make known to the Lord our needs—although He knows them before we even ask—but we ask Him to grant our prayer not in our terms but as He wills.

Because they are humble. Jewish elders went to Jesus to ask Him to cure the son of an official, a benefactor of the Jewish community. As Jesus and the elders were on their way to the official's house, the official sent his friends to say to Jesus, "Lord, do not trouble thyself, for I am not worthy that thou shouldst come under my roof, that is why <u>I did not think myself worthy to come to thee</u>. *But say the word and my servant will be healed.* For I, too, am a man subject to authority, and have soldiers subject to me. And I say to one, 'Go,' he goes and to my servant, 'Do this,' and he does it.' . . . And when the messenger returned to the official's home, they found the servant in good health" (Lk 7:1-10). When Jesus saw the official's humility, he marveled, saying, "Amen I say to you, I have not found such great faith in Israel" (Mt 8:10). Faith is rooted in humility. Without humility, one can't please God. Its opposite—pride—hurled Satan down to hell. Humility blossoms into faith. God does not like presumptuous prayers.

Because Mary intercedes. "And the wine having run short, <u>*the mother of Jesus said to him, 'They have no wine.'*</u> And Jesus said to her, 'What wouldst thou have me do, Woman? My hour has not yet come.' His mother said to the attendants, 'Do whatever he tells you.'" Following Jesus' command, *as Mary had told them,* the attendants filled the six stone water jars with water. And Jesus changed the water into wine (Jn 2:1-12). Our prayers to Mary instantly reach the ears of Jesus, her Son. *Ad Jesum per Mariam!* To Jesus through Mary!

Because they follow Jesus and the apostles. "'Rabboni, that I may see.' Jesus said to him, 'Go thy way. Thy faith has saved thee.' At once, he received his sight, and *followed him* along the road" (Mk 46-52). Lame from his mother's womb, he lay at the temple gate begging. When the two apostles saw him, Peter said, "Look at us." He looked at them, hoping to receive something from them, but Peter said, "Silver and gold I have none, but what I have, that I give thee. In the name of Jesus Christ of Nazareth, arise and walk." And taking him by the right hand, Peter raised him up, and immediately his feet became strong. Leaping up and praising God, *he went with them into the temple* (Acts 3:1-10). Jesus expects us to obey His wishes—even following Him up to Calvary—as expressions of our gratitude. Remember the ten lepers? Only one returned to thank Jesus for the cleansing miracle. May we not be among the nine!

Because they glorify God. When Jesus saw the stooped woman, He called her to him and said to her, "Woman, thou art delivered from thy infirmity. And He laid His hands upon her, and instantly she was made straight and *glorified God*" (Lk 13:10-16). Jesus cured a paralytic in Capharnaum. "And immediately he arose before them, took up what he had been lying on, and *went away to his house, glorifying God*" (Lk 5:25-26). We ask for things that glorify God, for things that are good for our souls, not for those that lead us to damnation. We must often examine our motives when asking for favors from God.

Why Relics?

Objects connected to Christ, the apostles, the Saints, and other holy persons have been revered and venerated as vehicles of God's power. In the gospels, the *Acts*, and the biographies of Saints, we read that miracles happened just through people touching or bringing the holy objects in contact with the sick or anyone in need of favors. These objects (including the bodies of the Saints) we call relics are in themselves powerless, but because they, having been connected to and in contact with the source of power (Christ, the apostles, the Saints), are sanctified, they become *conduits* of God's mercy for the good of mankind and for the glory of the Almighty Creator. (At the transfiguration, even the clothing that was connected to and in contact with Jesus shone with Him like the sun to reflect His glory.)

We keep in mind that just as the contact of the holy objects with their source of power that has sanctified them make them conduits, so does the contact—in fact, the *intimate union*—of the apostles and Saints with Christ has made them not only conduits but also *vessels of Christ's power.* Note that intimacy in St. Paul's words is "I live, no, not I but Christ lives in me." Ultimately, it is Christ *in* the Saints who performs miracles.

The hem of Jesus' cloak: When Jesus was on His way to Jairus' house to see his sick daughter, people followed Him and pressed Him. Instantly perceiving in Himself that power had gone forth from Him, he turned to the crowd and saw a woman, afraid, trembling, and falling down before Him. But he said to her, "Daughter, thy faith has saved thee. Go in peace, and be thou healed of thy affliction" (Mk 5:30-34). The woman had had a hemorrhage for twelve years and "suffered much at the hands of many physicians," spending all that she had yet finding no benefit. She had come up behind Jesus and touched the hem of his cloak, thinking, *If I touch but his cloak, I shall be saved.*

Performing miracles, Jesus laid His hands on the sick, used His voice to bring Lazarus and the widow's son of Naim back to life, and even used his spittle to bring back the sight to the man born blind.

St. Peter's shadow: "Now, by the hands of the Apostles, many signs and wonders were done . . . they carried the sick into the streets and laid them on beds so that when **Peter** passed, *his shadow at least might fall on some of them*" (Acts 5:12-16).

NICHOLAS LLANES ROSAL, STD, PHL, MSJ

St. Paul's handkerchiefs and aprons: "And God worked more than the usual miracle by the hand of **Paul,** so that *even handkerchiefs and aprons* were carried from his body to the sick, and *the diseases left them and the evil spirits went out"* (Acts 19:11-12).

St. Helena and the Cross: When the third cross was applied to the sick man, he was cured instantly. And St. Helena had the Shrine of the Holy Cross built on the spot where the cross was found.

Although *St. Augustine* was not said to have performed miracles during his lifetime, more than seventy miracles were credited to him after he brought the relic of *St. Stephen* to Hippo (*ES*).

When *Padre Pio* died, thousands went to see his body on display at his Rotondo convent chapel. People would just tear a small piece of his habit for a relic, prompting the friars to change his habit three times. Numerous miracles have been attributed to his intercession soon after his death (*ES*).

The *waters of Lourdes* were not found to have curative characteristics per se, but because of the Blessed Virgin's miraculous power and in consideration of St. Bernadette's sanctity, many miracles have been authenticated by the Vatican. Numerous favors were granted by the Blessed Mother in *Lourdes* and *Fátima* to devotees and other believers because God, out of His infinite goodness, wills them to happen. Miracles can happen anywhere as we saw where Jesus and the apostles performed them: in the temple, by the water, mountains, deserts, under the trees, on the streets, in homes, and in the hearts of people through . . .

Conversion: *St. Theodoret,* a priest of Antioch, built churches and chapels to house the relics of martyrs. Arrested by order of Emperor Julian the Apostate, the Saint was tormented on the rack as burning torches were applied to his bleeding wounds. "While enduring the pain, he raised his eyes to heaven and glorified God, asking that His name be honored forever. Hearing his prayer, the executioners fell to their knees and refused to apply the torches on the agonizing Saint. Converted to the Faith of the Saint, they were thrown into the river and drowned, and St. Theodoret was beheaded" (*ES*).

St. Hubert, grandson of Charibert, king of Toulouse, married the daughter of the count of Louvain. Raised in an environment of luxury, he ignored the observance of Good Friday and went with his friends to the chase. While chasing a stag, he saw the beast turn around and was surprised to see a crucifix between the antlers as a voice spoke, saying, "Hubert, unless you turn to the Lord and lead a holy life, you will go down to hell." He dismounted and kneeled down, saying, "Lord, what do you want me to do?" "Go seek Lambert," the voice replied. St. Lambert, the bishop of Maastricht, became his spiritual director. Shortly after, Hubert sold everything and studied to be a priest. When St. Lambert was killed by Pepin's followers, the pope appointed St. Hubert to succeed him. As bishop, he preached with so much unction that people flocked to listen to him. He converted many pagans. After a short illness, he died. He was proclaimed the Patron of Hunters (*HF*).

Miracles Teach Us a Way of Life

The teachings and miracles of Jesus, the edifying faith of the apostles, and the exemplary lives of Saints have given us a way of life to follow. We can tell how close our lives follow that way of life by the way we pray, for *the way we pray is the way we live,* and *the way we live is the way we pray.* We admire the effectiveness of the prayer of those who were healed because Christ answered their prayers with miracles. Trying to understand how their prayers were so effective, we gather that their prayers

> came out of a *clean heart* (Jesus forgave their sins: "Thy sins are forgiven thee").
>
> welled out of *humility* (centurion: "I did not think myself worthy to come to thee") that gave rise to an *unwavering faith* ("But say the word and my servant will be healed") rooted in love of God and neighbor ("And if I have faith so as to remove mountains yet not have love, I am nothing").

NICHOLAS LLANES ROSAL, STD, PHL, MSJ

expressed *resignation to the will of the Giver* ("Lord, if Thou wiliest, Thou canst make me clean" . . . "I will").

showed *willingness to follow Jesus* unto the end—even unto Calvary ("At once he received his sight and followed him" followed by Jesus' warning, "Sin no more").

begged for things intended to *give glory to God,* not for vain, ephemeral things (The paralytic "Immediately arose . . . and went away glorifying God").

If such be our prayer, then such be the life we aim to live: life in the state of grace that professes a humble, unwavering faith in Christ; a faith that is *rooted in love for God and neighbor;* love that is ever *resigned* to accept cheerfully and gratefully favors as well as trials from above; devotion to the welfare of our souls, not to the fleeting happiness on earth; and thanksgiving, adoration, and glory to Jesus and His mother now and forever. Amen.

APPENDIX I

The Canonization Process (*ES*)

THE CATHOLIC CHURCH does not make Saints except in the sense that, through the power of Christ and the Holy Spirit, it provides the means for people not only to live holy lives but also to reach the highest level of sanctity. Reaching that heroic level, persons, after their deaths, could prompt the church, after a thorough process, to proclaim them as Saints. (In the technical or canonical sense, there are no living saints.) In the early centuries of the church, a holy person was declared a Saint by acclamation.

As years went by, to ensure that the person that was honored as a Saint was truly worthy of the title and of the veneration accorded him or her as an intercessor, Pope Urban VIII in 1634 instituted a formal review of the life, faith, and morals of the candidate for sainthood to arrive at a reasonable basis to believe that the candidate was in heaven. If a miracle (which confirms a Saint's sanctity) was claimed to be the result of the candidate's intercession, a thorough examination was required to prove that divine intervention took place and that the miracle could not be explained by the laws of science. All the evidence was then reviewed by a panel of theologians, scientists, and other appropriate experts in the field. Except for some changes, the process instituted by Urban VIII continues to today's beatification and canonization processes.

Today, about sixty experts are said to be involved in that process, and if everything (candidate's authentic evidence of holiness and miracles) is found acceptable, a postulation follows, stating the authenticity of the candidate's eligibility for beatification or canonization. For beatification, one miracle is required; another is needed for canonization. The Congregation for the Causes of Saints then evaluates the postulation, and if approved, it goes to the pope who alone can beatify and canonize. By his supreme authority, the pope can speed up the process or put it on fast track and may even skip a miracle for canonization purposes.

Patron Saints (*ES*)

Academics, St. Thomas Aquinas

African Americans, St. Benedict the Moor

Art, St. Catherine of Bologna

Athletes, St. Sebastian

Aviators, St. Joseph Cupertino

Bachelors, St. Theobald

Bakers, St. Elizabeth of Hungary

Bishops, St. Ambrose

Blind People, St. Clare of Assisi

Broadcasters, St. Gabriel the Archangel

Bus Drivers, St. Christopher

Canonists, St. Raymond of Peñafort

Chastity, St. Agnes and St. Thomas Aquinas

Childbirth, St. Gerard Majella

The Church, St. Joseph

Computers, St. Isidore of Seville

Dentists, St. Apollonia

Difficult Marriages, St. Elizabeth of Portugal

Drivers, St. Fiacre

Editors, St. John Bosco

Accountants, St. Matthew the Apostle

Anglers, St. Andrew the Apostle

Architects, St. Thomas the Apostle

Authors, St. Mark the Evangelist

Babies, Holy Innocents

Bad Luck (against), St. Agricola

Beggars, St. Labre and St. Alexis

Blacks, St. Martin de Porres

Brides, St. Adelaide

Barbers, St. Martin de Porres

Cancer Victims, St. Bernard of Clairvaux

Catholic Youth, St. Aloysius Gonzaga

Chest Problems, St. Bernadine

Children, St. Maria Goretti

Composers, St. Cecilia

Cooks, St. Lawrence

Detraction, St. Nepomucene

Divine Intervention, St. Margaret

Dying People, St. James the Less

Elderly People, St. Anthony of Padua

Engaged Couples, St. Valentine

Eyes, St. Lucy of Syracuse

Families, St. Joseph

Fire, St. Agatha

Freemasons, Four Crowned Martyrs

Gambling (uncontrolled), St. Bernardino of Siena

Girls, St. Agnes of Rome

Handicapped People, St. Angela Merici

Happy Marriage, St. Valentine

Headache Sufferers, St. Teresa of Avila

Horses, St. Anthony of Padua

Impenitence, St. Jude

Infants, St. Nicholas Tolentino

Infidelity (against), St. Monica

Intestinal Diseases, St. Elmo

Jealousy, St. Elizabeth of Portugal

Knowledge, Holy Spirit

Laborers, St. Isidore

Lawyers, St. Thomas More and St. Ivo

Lightning (against), St. Alexis

Lovers, St. Raphael

Lungs and Chest, St. Bernadine

Martyrs, St. Agatha

Married Couples, St. Joseph

Messengers, St. Gabriel

Music, St. Cecilia

Newborn Babies, St. Brigid of Ireland

Officials, St. Thomas Becket

Orators, St. John Chrysostom

Painters, St. Luke the Evangelist

Engineers, St. Joseph

Expectant Mothers, St. Anthony

Farmers, St. Isidore

Firefighters, St. Florian

Forgotten Causes, St. Jude

Gardeners, St. Dorothy

Grooms, St. Louis IX

Grandmothers, St. Anne

Health Workers, St. Martin de Porres

Heart Patients, St. John of God

Impossible Cases, St. Jude

Impoverished, St. Martin de Porres

Infertility, St. Rita of Cascia

Insanity, St. Dymphna

Invalids, St. Roch

Journalists, St. Francis de Sales

Kidney Disease, St. Abinus

Lame People, St. Clotilde

Learning, St. Ambrose

Longevity, St. Peter

Lunatics, St. Christina and St. Dymphna

Maids, St. Zita

Marital Problems, St. Elizabeth of Portugal

Mathematics, St. Hubert

Missionaries, St. Therese

Nervous Diseases, St. Bartholomew the Apostle

Nurses, St. Agatha and St. Alexis

Old Maids, St. Andrew the Apostle

Orphans, St. Jerome Emiliani

Parents Separated from Children, St. Therese of Lisieux

Philosophers, St. Catherine of Alexandria

Poets, King David and St. Columba

Poor, St. Anthony of Padua

Preachers, St. John Chrysostom

Priests, St. John Vianney

Radio Workers, St. Gabriel the Archangel

Safe Journey, St. Raphael the Archangel

School Children, St. Albert the Great

Singers, St. Cecilia and St. Andrew the Apostle

Skin Diseases, St. Roch

Snakes, St. Patrick

Solitary Death, St. Francis of Assisi

Storms (against), St. Petroc

Students, St. Albert the Great

Tailors, St. Bartholomew the Apostle

Temptation, St. Michael the Archangel

Throat Diseases (against), St. Blaise

Travelers, St. Anthony of Padua and St. Christopher

Tuberculosis Sufferers, St. Pantaleon

Ulcers (against), St. Bartholomew the Apostle

Universities, St. Ferrini and St. Ignatius Loyola

Vocations, St. Alphonsus Ligouri

Widowers, St. Edgar

Women in Labor, St. Anne

Young Women, St. Ursula

Zoos, St. Francis of Assisi

Physicians, Sts. Cosmas and Damian

Police Officers, St. Michael the Archangel

Postal Workers, St. Gabriel the Archangel

Pregnant Women, St. Anne and St. Gerard

Race Relations, St. Martin de Porres

Salespeople, St. Lucy of Syracuse

Schools, St. Thomas Aquinas

Sick Children, St. Pharaildis

Single Mothers, St. Margaret of Cortona

Slander, St. John Nepomucene

Soldiers, St. Joan of Arc

Spinsters, St. Andrew the Apostle

Strokes (against), St. Andrew Avellino

Swimmers, St. Adjutor

Teachers, St. Catherine of Alexandria

Theologians, St. Augustine of Hippo

Toothache Sufferers, St. Apollonia

Truck Drivers, St. Christopher

Tumors, St. Rita of Cascia

Understanding, Holy Spirit

Virgins, St. Agnes of Rome

War, St. Elizabeth of Portugal

Widows, St. Adelaide and St. Clotilde

Writers, St. Francis de Sales

Youths, St. Aloysius Gonzaga

BIBLIOGRAPHY

Aquinatis, Sancti Thomae. *Summa Theologiae.* 5 vols. Biblioteca de Autores Cristianos, La Editorial Catolica, 1952.

Catechism of the Catholic Church. An Image Book. New York, New York: Doubleday, 1995.

Denzinger-Schönmetzer. *Enchiridion Symbolorum Definitionum et Declarationum de Rebus Fidei et Morum.* Barcinone, 1965.

Guiley, Rosemary Ellen. *The Encyclopedia of Saints.* New York, New York: Checkmark Books, 2001.

Hartman, Louis F. *Encyclopedic Dictionary of the Bible.* McGraw-Hill Book Company, 1963.

Jones, Alexander. *The New Testament of the Jerusalem Bible.* Garden City, New York: Doubleday, 1966.

Levy, Rosalie Marie. *Heavenly Friends.* St. Paul editions. Boston, Massachussetts, 1979.

Merk, Augustinus. *Novum Testamentum: Graece et Latine.* Romae: Instituti Biblici, 1948.

Orchard, Dom Bernard et al. *A Catholic Commentary on Holy Scripture.* Toronto: Thomas Nelson & Sons, 1951.

Rosal, Nicholas L. *Jerusalem Journal.* Quezon City, Philippines: Claretian Publications, 2009.

The Holy Bible. Confraternity Version. The American Catholic Edition. New York, New York: Benziger Brothers, 1962.

Wise, Michael et al. *Dead Sea Scrolls.* Harper San Francisco, 1996.

Woodward, Kenneth. *The Book of Miracles.* New York, New York: Simon & Schuster, 2000.

INDEX

ABOUT THE AUTHOR

 Dr. Nicholas L. Rosal taught Christology and moral theology at St. Francis College in Brooklyn and at the former Brooklyn campus of St. John's University. Before moving to Brooklyn, he was an adjunct theology professor at the Loyola University in Chicago while attending journalism classes at Northwestern University in Evanston, Illinois. He also worked in the Spanish parish of St. Anthony in Gary, Indiana. A preacher for the propagation of the faith under then-bishop Fulton J. Sheen, he has given retreats to nuns and recollections to priests.

He earned his doctoral degree in theology at the Pontifical Seminary of the University of Santo Tomas in Manila, a licentiate in philosophy at the same university, and a master's degree in journalism at Northwestern. In addition to writing numerous articles about religious, educational, and government issues, he has published pamphlets on ecumenism and written books, including *The Jerusalem Journal*, a continuous story of Jesus' life, and *The Unjust Position of the Church in the Philippine Constitution*, a study of the church-state relations in the predominantly Catholic country in Asia. He also wrote *An Exotic Language: Ilokano* (available at Amazon), a linguistic analysis of one of the major Philippine languages (on top of over one hundred Philippine dialects). He has translated from English to Ilocano the entire *Catechism of the Catholic Church*, a voluminous work now in the hands of the archbishop of Nueva Segovia. The author has also written an unpublished *Life of Christ* in his native language.

Before coming to the United States, he held briefly the position of chancellor and director of Student Catholic Action of the Nueva Segovia Archdiocese (Vigan City). He also taught Latin, religion, and music at the archdiocese's minor seminary. Asked by Father Rector Juan Ylla, a renowned canonist, he composed a Latin mass for the Pontifical Seminary Choir in honor of St. Raymond of Peñafort, canon law's patron saint.

After he received permission from the Vatican to leave the ministry, he went to work as an education advocate for the Perth Amboy City Board of Education in New Jersey. He subsequently became director of the board's Adult and Continuing Education Department and principal of the Bilingual Adult High School. As a community volunteer, he moderated for twenty years a public call-in radio program (WCTC) and cofounded the St. Matthew's Philippine-American Association of Edison, New Jersey. In the Philippines for a few months in 2009-2010, he was given a broadcast hour on the Nueva Segovia Radio (963 AM) four days a week, discussing ecumenism-related issues. He continues today to contribute broadcast materials for the station.

Dr. Rosal, one of eleven siblings, was born in San Vicente, Ilocos Sur, Philippines, to devout Catholic parents (Alfonso, a lawyer, and Matilde, a schoolteacher). The author has three sons (Anthony Nicholas, Patrick, and Mark) from his marriage to Mimi (deceased) and a stepdaughter (Christine) by his marriage to Thelma.

Edwards Brothers Malloy
Thorofare, NJ USA
December 5, 2013